Internet and World Wide Web

Simplified®, 2nd Edition

IDG's **3-D Visual** Series

IDG Books Worldwide, Inc.
An International Data Group Company
Foster City, CA • Indianapolis • Chicago • Dallas

Internet and World Wide Web Simplified®, 2nd Edition

Published by
IDG Books Worldwide, Inc.
An International Data Group Company
919 E. Hillsdale Blvd., Suite 400
Foster City, CA 94404

Library of Congress Catalog Card No.:
ISBN: 0-7645-6029-8

Printed in the United States of America
10 9 8 7 6 5 4 3 2 1

XX/XX/XX/XX/XX

Distributed in the United States by IDG Books Worldwide, Inc.

Distributed by Transworld Publishers Limited in the United Kingdom and Europe; by WoodsLane Pty. Ltd. for Australia; by WoodsLane Enterprises Ltd. for New Zealand; by Longman Singapore Publishers Ltd. for Singapore, Malaysia, Thailand, and Indonesia; by Simron Pty. Ltd. for South Africa; by Toppan Company Ltd. for Japan; by Distribuidora Cuspide for Argentina; by Livraria Cultura for Brazil; by Ediciencia S.A. for Ecuador; by Addison-Wesley Publishing Company for Korea; by Ediciones ZETA S.C.R. Ltda. for Peru; by WS Computer Publishing Company, Inc., for the Philippines; by Unalis Corporation for Taiwan; by Contemporanea de Ediciones for Venezuela. Authorized Sales Agent: Anthony Rudkin Associates for the Middle East and North Africa.

For general information on IDG Books Worldwide's books in the U.S., please call our Consumer Customer Service department at 800-762-2974. For reseller information, including discounts and premium sales, please call our Reseller Customer Service department at 800-434-3422.

For information on where to purchase IDG Books Worldwide's books outside the U.S., please contact our International Sales department at 415-655-3023 or fax 415-655-3299.

For information on foreign language translations, please contact our Foreign & Subsidiary Rights department at 415-655-3021 or fax 415-655-3281.

For sales inquiries and special prices for bulk quantities, please contact our Sales department at 415-655-3200 or write to the address above.

For information on using IDG Books Worldwide's books in the classroom or for ordering examination copies, please contact our Educational Sales department at 800-434-2086 or fax 817-251-8174.

For press review copies, author interviews, or other publicity information, please contact our Public Relations department at 415-655-3000 or fax 415-655-3299.

For authorization to photocopy items for corporate, personal, or educational use, please contact Copyright Clearance Center, 222 Rosewood Drive, Danvers, MA 01923, or fax 508-750-4470.

Trademark Acknowledgments

©1997
maranGraphics, Inc.

The animated characters are the copyright of maranGraphics, Inc.

U.S. Corporate Sales	**U.S. Trade Sales**
Contact maranGraphics at (800) 469-6616 or Fax (905) 890-9434.	Contact IDG Books at (800) 434-3422 or (415) 655-3000.

Welcome to the world of IDG Books Worldwide.

IDG Books Worldwide, Inc., is a subsidiary of International Data Group, the world's largest publisher of computer-related information and the leading global provider of information services on information technology. IDG was founded more than 25 years ago and now employs more than 8,500 people worldwide. IDG publishes more than 270 computer publications in over 75 countries (see listing below). More than 90 million people read one or more IDG publications each month.

Launched in 1990, IDG Books Worldwide is today the #1 publisher of best-selling computer books in the United States. We are proud to have received eight awards from the Computer Press Association in recognition of editorial excellence and three from Computer Currents' First Annual Readers' Choice Awards. Our best-selling ...For Dummies® series has more than 25 million copies in print with translations in 30 languages. IDG Books Worldwide, through a joint venture with IDG's Hi-Tech Beijing, became the first U.S. publisher to publish a computer book in the People's Republic of China. In record time, IDG Books Worldwide has become the first choice for millions of readers around the world who want to learn how to better manage their businesses.

Our mission is simple: Every one of our books is designed to bring extra value and skill-building instructions to the reader. Our books are written by experts who understand and care about our readers. The knowledge base of our editorial staff comes from years of experience in publishing, education, and journalism - experience which we use to produce books for the '90s. In short, we care about books, so we attract the best people. We devote special attention to details such as audience, interior design, use of icons, and illustrations. And because we use an efficient process of authoring, editing, and desktop publishing our books electronically, we can spend more time ensuring superior content and spend less time on the technicalities of making books.

You can count on our commitment to deliver high-quality books at competitive prices on topics you want to read about. At IDG Books Worldwide, we continue in the IDG tradition of delivering quality for more than 25 years. You'll find no better book on a subject than one from IDG Books Worldwide.

John Kilcullen
President and CEO
IDG Books Worldwide, Inc.

IDG Books Worldwide, Inc., is a subsidiary of International Data Group, the world's largest publisher of computer-related information and the leading global provider of information services on information technology. International Data Group publishes over 276 computer publications in over 75 countries. Ninety million people read one or more International Data Group publications each month. International Data Group's publications include: Argentina: Annuario de Informatica, Computerworld Argentina, PC World Argentina; Australia: Australian Macworld, Client/Server Journal, Computer Living, Computerworld, Computerworld 100, Digital News, IT Casebook, Network World, On-line World Australia, PC World, Publishing Essentials, Reseller, WebMaster; Austria: Computerwelt Osterreich, Networks Austria, PC Tip; Belarus: PC World Belarus; Belgium: Data News; Brazil: Annuário de Informática, Computerworld Brazil, Connections, Super Game Power, Macworld, PC Player, PC World Brazil, Publish Brazil, Reseller News; Bulgaria: Computerworld Bulgaria, Networkworld/Bulgaria, PC & MacWorld Bulgaria; Canada: CIO Canada, Client/Server World, ComputerWorld Canada, InfoCanada, Network World Canada; Chile: Computerworld Chile, PC World Chile; Colombia: Computerworld Colombia, PC World Colombia, Costa Rica: PC World Centro America; The Czech and Slovak Republics: Computerworld Czechoslovakia, Elektronika Czechoslovakia, Macworld Czech Republic, PC World Czechoslovakia; Denmark: Communications World, Computerworld Danmark, Macworld Danmark, PC Privat Danmark, PC World Danmark, PC World Danmark Supplements, TECH World; Dominican Republic: PC World Republica Dominicana; Ecuador: PC World Ecuador; Egypt: Computerworld Middle East, PC World Middle East; El Salvador: PC World Centro America; Finland: MikroPC, Tietoverkko, Tietoviikko; France: Distributique, Golden, Hebdo-Distributique, Info PC, Le Guide du Monde Informatique, Le Monde Informatique, Reseaux & Telecoms; Germany: Computer Partner, Computerwoche, Computerwoche Extra, Computerwoche Focus, I/M Information Management, Macwelt, PC Welt; Greece: GamePro, Multimedia World; Guatemala: PC World Centro America; Honduras: PC World Centro America; Hong Kong: Computerworld Hong Kong, PCWorld Hong Kong, Publish in Asia; Hungary: ABCD CD-ROM, Computerworld Szamitastechnika, PC & Mac World Hungary, PC-X Magazine; Iceland: Tolvuheimur/PC World Island; India: Information Systems Computerworld, PC World India, Publish in Asia; Indonesia: InfoKomputer PC World, Komputek Computerworld, Publish in Asia; Ireland: ComputerScope, PC Live!; Israel: People & Computers; Italy: Computerworld Italia, Computerworld Italia Special Editions, Macworld Italia, Networking Italia, PC Shopping, PC World Italia, PC World/Walt Disney; Japan: DTP World, HP Open World Japan, Macworld Japan, Nikkei Personal Computing, Open World Japan, OS/2 World Japan, SunWorld Japan, Windows World Japan; Kenya: East African Computer News; Korea: Hi-Tech Information/Computerworld, Macworld Korea, PC World Korea; Macedonia: PC World Macedonia; Malaysia: Computerworld Malaysia, PC World Malaysia, Publish in Asia; Mexico: Computerworld Mexico, Macworld, PC World Mexico; Myanmar: PC World Myanmar; Netherlands: Computer! Totaal, LAN Magazine, LanWorld Buyers Guide, Macworld, Net Magazine, Totaal! Beurskrant; New Zealand: Absolute Beginner's Guide, Computer Buyer, Computer Industry Directory, Computerworld New Zealand, MTB, Network World, PC World New Zealand; Nicaragua: PC World Centro America; Nigeria: PC World Nigeria; Norway: Computerworld Norge, Computerworld Privat (Datamagasinet), CW Rapport Norge, IDG's KURSGUIDE, Macworld Norge, Multimediaworld, PC World Ekspress, PC World Nettverk, PC World Norge, PC World's Produktguide, Windows World Spesial; Pakistan: Computerworld Pakistan, PC World Pakistan; Panama: PC World Panama; P. R. of China: China Computer Users, China Computerworld, China Infoworld, China Telecom World Weekly; Computer & Communication, Electronic Design China, Electronics Today, Electronics Weekly, Game Camp, Game Soft, Network World China, PC World China, Popular Computer Weekly, Software Weekly, Software World, Telecom World; Peru: Computerworld Peru, PC World Profesional Peru, PC World Peru; Poland: Computerworld Poland, Computerworld Special Report, Macworld, Networld, PC World Komputer; Philippines: Computerworld Philippines, PC World Philippines, Publish in Asia; Portugal: Cerebro/PC World, Computerworld/Correio Informático, Dealer World Portugal, Mac*In/PC*In, Multimedia World Portugal; Puerto Rico: PC World Puerto Rico; Romania: Computerworld Romania, PC World Romania, Telecom Romania; Russia: Computerworld Russia, Mir PK, Sety; Singapore: Computerworld Singapore, PC World Singapore, Publish in Asia; Slovenia: MONITOR; South Africa: Computing S.A., InfoWorld S.A., Network World S.A., Software World; Spain: Computerworld Espa-a, COMUNICACIONES WORLD, Dealer World, Macworld Espa-a, PC World Espa-a; Sweden: CAP&Design, Computer Sweden, Corporate Computing, MacWorld, Maxi Data, MikroDatorn, Nätverk & Kommunikation, PC/Aktiv, PC World, Windows World; Switzerland: Computerworld Schweiz, Macworld Schweiz, PCtip; Taiwan: Computerworld Taiwan, Macworld Taiwan, PC World Taiwan, Publish Taiwan, Windows World; Thailand: Thai Computerworld, Publish in Asia; Turkey: Computerworld Turkiye, MACWORLD Turkiye, PC WORLD Turkiye; Ukraine: Computerworld Kiev, Computers & Software, Multimedia World Ukraine, PC World Ukraine; United Kingdom: Acorn User, Amiga Action, Amiga Computing, Appletalk, Computing, GamePro, Macworld, Network News, Parents and Computers, PC Advisor, PC Home, PSX Pro UK, The WEB; United States: Cable in the Classroom, CD Review, CIO Magazine, Computerworld, Computerworld Client/Server Journal, Digital Video Magazine, DOS World, Federal Computer Week, GamePro, InfoWorld, I-Way, JavaWorld, Macworld, Multimedia World, Netscape World Online, Network World, PC Entertainment, PC World, Publish, SunWorld Online, SWATPro Magazine, Video Event, WebMaster; Uruguay: PC World Uruguay; Venezuela: Computerworld Venezuela, PC World Venezuela; and Vietnam: PC World Vietnam.

*Every maranGraphics book represents
the extraordinary vision and commitment of a unique family:
the Maran family of Toronto, Canada.*

Back Row (from left to right): *Sherry Maran, Rob Maran, Richard Maran, Maxine Maran, Jill Maran.*
Front Row (from left to right): *Judy Maran, Ruth Maran.*

Richard Maran is the company founder and its inspirational leader. He developed maranGraphics' proprietary communication technology called "visual grammar." This book is built on that technology—empowering readers with the easiest and quickest way to learn about computers.

Ruth Maran is the Author and Architect—a role Richard established that now bears Ruth's distinctive touch. She creates the words and visual structure that are the basis for the books.

Judy Maran is the Project Coordinator. She works with Ruth, Richard and the highly talented maranGraphics illustrators, designers and editors to transform Ruth's material into its final form.

Rob Maran is the Technical and Production Specialist. He makes sure the state-of-the-art technology used to create these books always performs as it should.

Sherry Maran manages the Reception, Order Desk and any number of areas that require immediate attention and a helping hand.

Jill Maran is a jack-of-all-trades and dynamo who fills in anywhere she's needed anytime she's back from university.

Maxine Maran is the Business Manager and family sage. She maintains order in the business and family—and keeps everything running smoothly.

Oh, and three other family members are seated on the sofa. These graphic disk characters help make it fun and easy to learn about computers. They're part of the extended maranGraphics family.

Credits

Authors:
Paul Whitehead
Ruth Maran

Copy Development:
Kelleigh Wing

Copy Development of Updated Sections:
Brad Hilderley

Development of Web Site Section:
Jill Maran

Project Coordinator:
Judy Maran

Editors:
Peter Lejcar
Tina Veltri

Proofreader and Screen Shot Permissions:
Roxanne Coppens

Layout Designers:
Ben Lee
Jamie Bell
Christie Van Duin

Illustrations:
Chris K.C. Leung
Russell Marini
Jeff Jones

Indexer:
Kelleigh Wing

Post Production:
Robert Maran

Acknowledgments

Thanks to the dedicated staff of maranGraphics, including Carol Barclay, Jamie Bell, Roxanne Coppens, Francisco Ferreira, Brad Hilderley, Jeff Jones, Wanda Lawrie, Ben Lee, Treena Lees, Peter Lejcar, Chris K.C. Leung, Michael W. MᵃᶜDonald, Jill Maran, Judy Maran, Maxine Maran, Robert Maran, Russ Marini, Tina Veltri, Paul Whitehead and Kelleigh Wing.

Finally, to Richard Maran who originated the easy-to-use graphic format of this guide. Thank you for your inspiration and guidance.

Screen Shot Permissions

Screens Appearing Throughout the Book

AltaVista screen shots used with permission. AltaVista, the AltaVista logo, and the Digital logo are trademarks of Digital Equipment Corporation.

Eudora Light screen shots used with permission. Eudora® is a registered trademark of QUALCOMM Incorporated.

Macintosh operating system screens and equipment used with permission. Macintosh is a registered trademark of Apple Computer, Inc.

Excite, WebCrawler, Excite City.Net, City.Net, the Excite Logo and the WebCrawler Logo are trademarks of Excite, Inc. and may be registered in various jurisdictions. Excite screen display copyright 1995-1997 Excite, Inc.

Microsoft operating screen, Microsoft Network Today and Microsoft Internet Explorer all reprinted by permission of Microsoft Corporation.

Netscape screens used with permission. Netscape and Netscape Navigator are trademarks of Netscape Communications Corp.

Shareware.com screens reprinted with permission from CNET, Inc., copyright 1995-7. www.cnet.com

Yahoo screen shots used with permission. Text and artwork copyright © 1996 by YAHOO!, Inc. All rights reserved. YAHOO! and the YAHOO! logo are trademarks of YAHOO!, Inc.

Chapter 1

America Online screen used with permission. Copyright 1996-97 America Online, Inc. All Rights Reserved.

CompuServe screen shot used with permission.

Chapter 2

New Balance Cyberpark USA used with permission.

Spiegel. Copyright Spiegel Inc. Used by permission.

Empire Mall screen shots used with permission.

Flower Stop screen shots used with permission.

Back-Trac Records. Logo cannot be copied or retransmitted without the express written permission of Back-Trac Records. Logo and the trade names of BTR copyrighted and property of BTR.

Surfermag.com. All photos on the Surfermag.com Web site are copyrighted and may not be used on other Web sites or other media without expressed written consent of SURFER Publications or the photographers themselves.

The Complete Works of William Shakespeare used with permission.

Le Grand Louvre Mona Lisa screen shot used with permission.

Cybertown images copyright Cybertown 1996.

Reprinted by permission. Infoseek, Ultraseek, Quickseek, Ultrashop, "proof of intelligent life on the net" and the Infoseek logos are trademarks of Infoseek Corporation which may be registered in certain jurisdictions. Other trademarks shown are trademarks of their respective owners. Copyright © 1995-1997 Infoseek Corporation. All rights reserved.

The Lycos "Catalog of the Internet" Copyright © 1994-1997 Carnegie Mellon University. All rights reserved. Lycos is a trademark of Carnegie Mellon University. Used by permission.

Submit It! Screen used with permission.

WebTV screens used with permission.

Chapter 6

Ircle screen used with permission.

mIRC screen used with permission.

PIRCH screen used with permission.

ichat screen used with permission.

WebChat Broadcasting System used with permission.

Chapter 7

Library of Congress FTP screens used with permission.

Windows 'Error' screen used with permission.

ArchiePlexForm used with permission.

Animals

Electronic Zoo screen shot used with permission.

Turtle Trax screen used by permission. Ursula Keuper-Bennett and Peter Bennett retain all rights to the text and images contained within Turtle Trax.

Art

Kaleidospace screen used with permission.

Astronomy

Shuttle Web screen used with permission.

Biology

Institute for Molecular Virology screen used with permission.

Bizarre

Contortion Home Page screen used with permission.

Monkeys Typing Shakespeare screen used with permission.

Books and Language

Amazon.com screen used with permission. Amazon.com site as of June 25, 1997 reprinted by permission of Amazon.com.

Business: Companies

Crayola screen shot used by permission.

JCPenney screen shot used with permission. © 1997 J.C. Penney Company, Inc. and/or JCP Media Corporation. All Rights Reserved.

Ragu screen shot used with permission.

Business: Finance

Citibank screen used with permission.

Image used by permission of The Principal Financial Group. All Rights Reserved. Copyright 1997 The Principal Financial Group. All Rights Reserved.

Business: Shopping

Internet Shopping Network screen used with permission.

Cars

DealerNET screen used with permission.

Saturn screen shot: © Saturn Corporation, used with permission.

Chemistry

DuPont screen used with permission. Copyright © 1995, 1996, 1997 E. I. du Pont de Nemours and Company. All Rights Reserved.

Computers: Pictures

Clip Art Connection screen used with permission.

Time Life Photo Site screen used with permission. Design by Marthe Smith. Copyright Time Inc.

Computers: Resources

Adobe. Copyright 1996, Adobe Systems, Inc.

Novell. The contents of Novell World Wide are protected by the copyright laws of the United States. No portion may be reproduced in any form, or by any means, without the prior written consent of Novell, Inc.

TUCOWS screen used with permission.

Computers: Sounds

Movie Sounds Page screen used with permission.

Dance

CyberDance - Ballet on the Net screen used with permission.
Information Super Dance Floor used by permission of Don Deyne.

Education

fastWEB screen used with permission.
Kids' Space. Copyright 1995-1997 Kids' Space ™. All rights reserved.

Environment and Weather

Rainforest Action Network screen used with permission.

Food and Drink

Gumbo Pages screen used with permission.
Pasta Home Page screen used with permission.

Games

Dogz screen used with permission.

Geography

City.Net screen used with permission.

Government and Information on the U.S.

U.S. Census Bureau screen used with permission.
Federal Courts' Home Page screen used with permission.

Government and Information on the World

Europa screen used with permission.
South African Government of National Unity screen used with permission.

Health

Eli Lilly and Company. Copyright © 1997 Eli Lilly and Company. All rights reserved.
Virtual Hospital. The Virtual Hospital ® is a registered trademark of The University of Iowa. All information contained within The Virtual Hospital is Copyright © 1992-1997 The University of Iowa, unless otherwise noted.

History

Gail Dedrick's Guide to the Monarchs of England and Great Britain screen used with permission.
World War I - Trenches on the Web screen used with permission.

Humor

Ask Dr. Science screen used with permission.
Laurel and Hardy screen used by permission.

Internet Resources

Cool Site of the Day is a trademark of InfiNet.
Magic URL Mystery Trip screen used with permission.

Jobs

Career Mosaic screen used with permission.

Macintosh

Apple Technical Support and Power Macintosh screens used with permission. Copyright Apple Computer Inc.

Magazines

Pathfinder. © 1997 Time Inc. New Media. All rights reserved. Reproduction in whole or in part without permission is prohibited. Pathfinder is a registered trademark of Time Inc. New Media.

Movies

Drew's Scripts-O-Rama screen used with permission.
Internet Movie Database screen used with permission.
MovieWEB screen used with permission.

Museums

The Computer Network Museum screen used with permission.

Music

Cdnow. Copyright 1996 CDnow, Inc.
JAZZ Online® screen used with permission.

News

CNET: The Computer Network. Reprinted with permission from CNET Inc. Copyright, © 1995-7.
Comic Strip used with permission. Copyright © Newspaper Enterprise Association, Inc. and United Feature Syndicate, Inc. All rights reserved.

Religion

The Bible Gateway screen used with permission.

Search Tools

WebCrawler screen used with permission.

Sports

Skydive! screen used with permission.
TSN screen used with permission.

Television

Discovery Channel screen used with permission.
iQVC Shop screen used with permission.
The Weather Channel © 1997. Used with permission.

Theatre

Kabuki for Everyone screen used with permission.

Travel

Epicurious Travel screen used with permission.
Travel Source screen used with permission.

Windows

Windows95.com screen used with permission.

Table of Contents

CHAPTER 3

Electronic Mail

CHAPTER 4

Mailing Lists

CHAPTER 5

Newsgroups

Table of Contents

CHAPTER 9

Interesting Web Sites

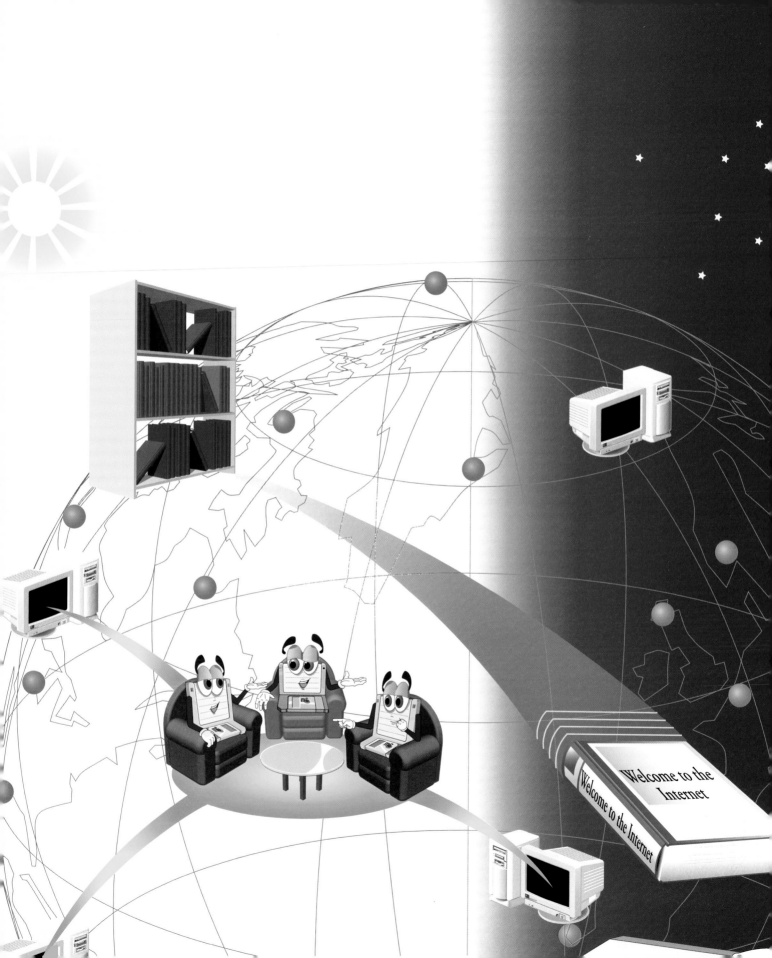

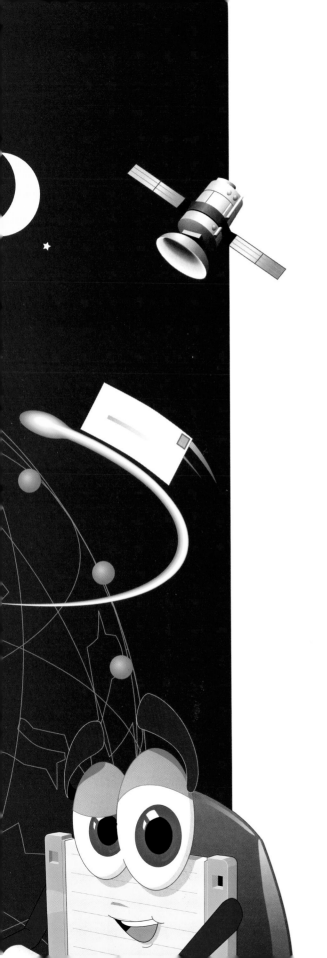

CHAPTER 1

THE INTERNET

What is the Internet? In this chapter you will learn what the Internet is, what it has to offer and how information transfers to your computer from sites around the world.

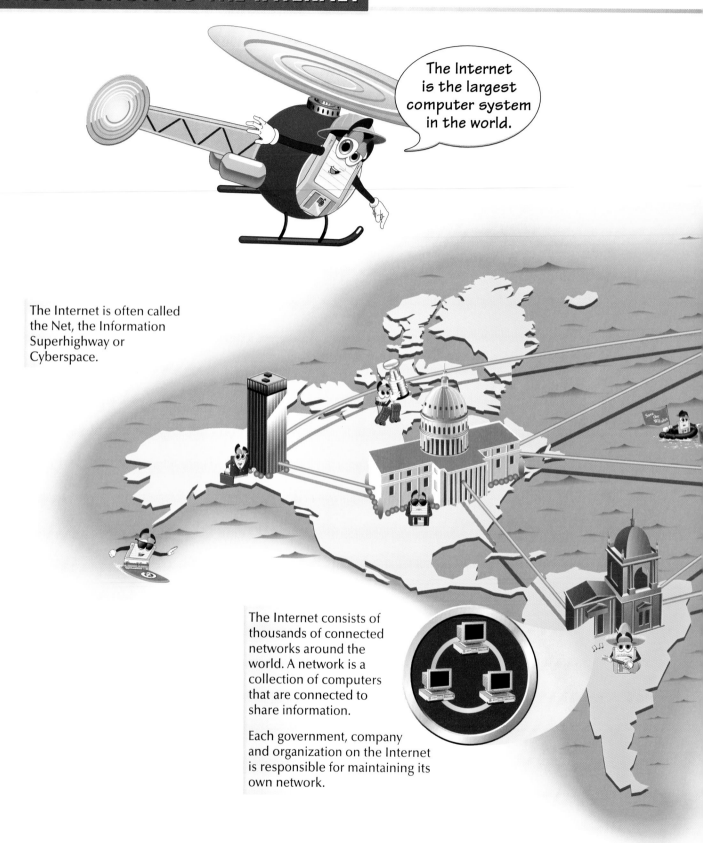

The Internet is the largest computer system in the world.

The Internet is often called the Net, the Information Superhighway or Cyberspace.

The Internet consists of thousands of connected networks around the world. A network is a collection of computers that are connected to share information.

Each government, company and organization on the Internet is responsible for maintaining its own network.

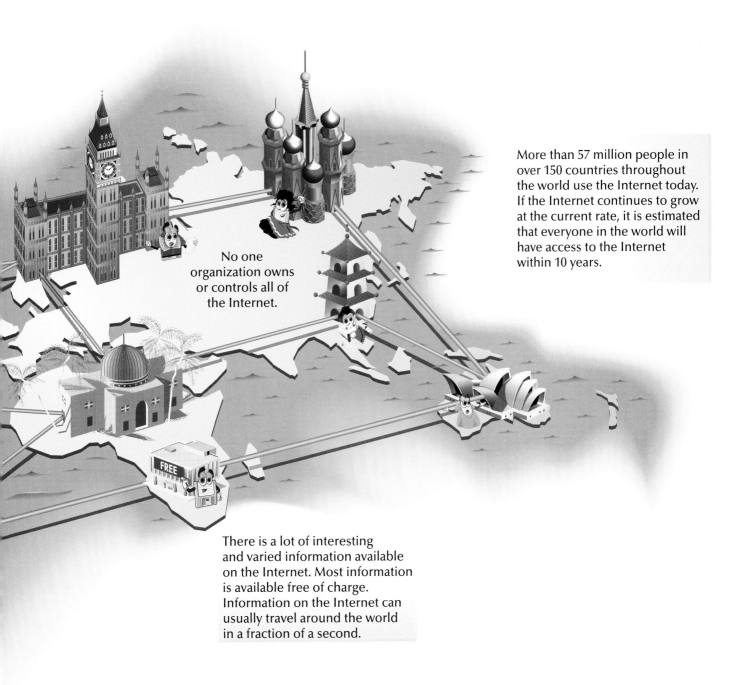

More than 57 million people in over 150 countries throughout the world use the Internet today. If the Internet continues to grow at the current rate, it is estimated that everyone in the world will have access to the Internet within 10 years.

No one organization owns or controls all of the Internet.

There is a lot of interesting and varied information available on the Internet. Most information is available free of charge. Information on the Internet can usually travel around the world in a fraction of a second.

WHAT THE INTERNET OFFERS

ELECTRONIC MAIL

Exchanging electronic mail (e-mail) is the most popular feature on the Internet. You can exchange electronic mail with people around the world, including friends, colleagues, family members, customers and even people you meet on the Internet. Electronic mail is fast, easy, inexpensive and saves paper.

INFORMATION

The Internet gives you access to information on any subject imaginable. You can review newspapers, magazines, academic papers, government documents, television show transcripts, famous speeches, recipes, job listings, works by Shakespeare, airline schedules and much more.

PROGRAMS

Thousands of programs are available on the Internet. These programs include word processors, spreadsheets, games and much more.

ENTERTAINMENT

Hundreds of simple games are available on the Internet, including backgammon, chess, poker, football and much more.

The Internet also lets you review current movies, listen to television theme songs, read movie scripts and have interactive conversations with people around the world—even celebrities.

DISCUSSION GROUPS

You can join discussion groups on the Internet to meet people around the world with similar interests. You can ask questions, discuss problems and read interesting stories.

There are thousands of discussion groups on topics such as the environment, food, humor, music, pets, photography, politics, religion, sports and television.

ONLINE SHOPPING

You can order goods and services on the Internet without ever leaving your desk. You can buy items such as books, computer programs, flowers, music CDs, pizza, stocks, used cars and much more.

There are no long-distance charges when you send or receive information on the Internet.

The Internet is made up of thousands of networks that belong to businesses, government agencies, colleges and universities around the world. These organizations pay to set up and maintain their own parts of the Internet.

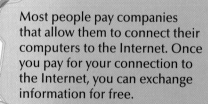

Most people pay companies that allow them to connect their computers to the Internet. Once you pay for your connection to the Internet, you can exchange information for free.

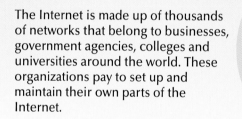

When you send information across the Internet, these organizations allow the information to pass through their networks free of charge. This lets you avoid long-distance charges.

WHO OFFERS FREE INFORMATION

Governments

Governments offer information such as federal budgets and NASA reports to educate the public.

Colleges and Universities

Colleges and universities make information such as journals and software available to the public.

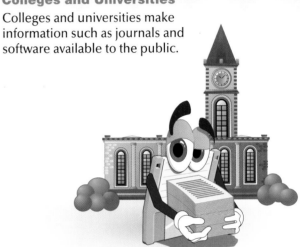

Companies

Companies offer free information to promote a good reputation and to interest you in their products. For example, Ford offers information about its cars and trucks on the Internet.

Individuals

Individuals around the world offer information to give something back to the community. For example, one individual offers dozens of television theme songs that you can access and listen to for free on the Internet.

The Internet was created by combining the ideas and talents of many people. Organizations and individuals have worked together for many years to make the Internet the valuable resource it is today.

ARPANET

In the late 1960s, the U.S. Defense Department created a network that linked military computers together. The network, called ARPANET, was connected in a way that ensured if one section of the network was damaged, the remaining computers on the network would still be able to communicate with each other.

NSFNET

The National Science Foundation created NSFNET in the mid-1980s. NSFNET used the technology developed for ARPANET to allow universities and schools to connect to each other. By 1987, NSFNET could no longer handle the amount of information that was being transferred. The National Science Foundation improved the network to allow more information to transfer. This improved, high-speed network became the Internet.

Public Access

In the 1980s, most of the people accessing the Internet were scientists and researchers. In the early 1990s, many companies started to offer access to home users. This allowed anyone with a modem and a computer to access the Internet.

The World Wide Web

The World Wide Web was created in the early 1990s by the European Laboratory for Particle Physics. The goal of the World Wide Web was to allow researchers to work together on projects and to make project information easily accessible. The first publicly accessible Web site was created in 1993.

Commercial Sites

By the mid-1990s, over 30 million people had access to the Internet. To reach this huge market, most big companies created their own sites on the World Wide Web to sell or provide information about their products. There are now thousands of companies on the Web.

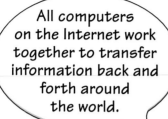

All computers on the Internet work together to transfer information back and forth around the world.

Packets

When you send information through the Internet, the information is broken down into smaller pieces, called packets. Each packet travels independently through the Internet and may take a different path to arrive at the intended destination.

When information arrives at its destination, the packets are reassembled.

TCP/IP

Transmission Control Protocol/Internet Protocol (TCP/IP) is a language computers on the Internet use to communicate with each other. TCP/IP divides information you send into packets and sends the packets across the Internet. When information arrives at the intended destination, TCP/IP ensures that all the packets arrived safely.

Backbone

The backbone of the Internet is a set of high-speed data lines that connect major networks all over the world.

Router

A router is a specialized device that regulates traffic on the Internet and picks the most efficient route for each packet. A packet may pass through many routers before reaching its intended destination.

Download and Upload Information

When you receive information from another computer on the Internet, you are downloading the information.

When you send information to another computer on the Internet, you are uploading the information.

THE FUTURE OF THE INTERNET

The Internet is growing and changing at an extraordinary rate. In the future, there will be new ways to access the Internet and different types of information available.

High-Speed Access

Most people who access the Internet from home use a modem. Modems are a very slow way to transfer information. Eventually, most people will have much faster access to the Internet. High-speed access will allow users to watch movies or listen to CD-quality sound on the Internet.

Automatic Information Retrieval

Most information on the Internet is poorly organized. Searching for information on a specific topic requires you to use a number of programs and search tools to get the information. In the future, programs will exist that will automatically find and retrieve information of interest. By analyzing the type of information you read, the program will be able to make decisions about what information to retrieve for you.

Users

There are approximately 57 million people on the Internet. By the year 2000, there could be over 400 million people on the Internet. This will make the Internet an even more valuable source for diverse and interesting information.

Virtual Reality

Virtual reality is a computer-generated, three-dimensional world. Virtual reality software allows you to enter a virtual reality world and interact with images. In the future, many resources on the Internet will use virtual reality. You will be able to walk through shopping malls or even visit other planets without ever leaving your home.

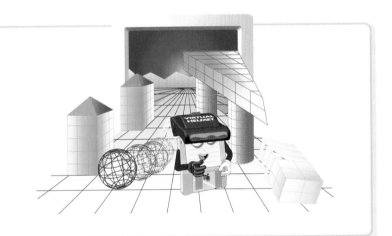

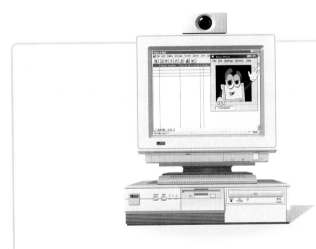

Video E-Mail

Instead of typing e-mail messages to your friends and colleagues, you will eventually be able to record a video and send it to them over the Internet. When your friends and colleagues check their e-mail, they will be able to view the video you sent.

GETTING CONNECTED

You need specific equipment
and programs to connect to
the Internet.

COMPUTER

You can use any type of computer,
such as an IBM-compatible or
Macintosh computer, to connect
to the Internet.

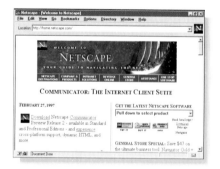

PROGRAMS

You need special programs to use
the Internet. Most companies that
connect you to the Internet provide
the programs you need free of charge.

MODEM

You need a modem to connect to the
Internet. Choose a modem with a
speed of at least 28,800 bps, although
a modem with a speed of 56,000 bps is
recommended.

WAYS TO CONNECT

Connection Service

An Internet Service Provider (ISP) or commercial online service can connect you to the Internet for a fee.

Make sure you choose a connection service with a local telephone number to avoid long-distance charges.

Freenets

A freenet is a free, local service that provides community information and access to the Internet. Most freenets do not let you see images, so you can only view text on your screen.

Freenets can be difficult to connect to because they are often busy.

USER NAME AND PASSWORD

You have to enter a user name and password when you want to connect to the Internet. This ensures that you are the only one who can access your Internet account.

Choosing a Password

When choosing a password, do not use words that people can easily associate with you, such as your name or favorite sport. The most effective password connects two words or number sequences with a special character (example: blue@123). You should never write down your password in case someone else sees the password.

INTERNET SERVICE PROVIDER

An Internet Service Provider (ISP) is a company that gives you access to the Internet for a fee.

Cost

There are different ways an Internet service provider can charge you for the time you spend on the Internet. Many service providers offer you a certain number of hours per day or month for a set fee. If you exceed the total number of hours, you are usually charged for every extra hour.

Some ISPs offer unlimited access to the Internet for a flat fee. Make sure you are aware of any hidden charges or restrictions.

Some service providers charge a fee for setting up your connection to the Internet.

Busy Signals

Ask the service provider how many members there are for each phone line. More than ten members for each phone line means you may get a busy signal when you try to connect.

INTERNET SERVICE PROVIDER FEATURES

Getting Help

Setting up a connection to an Internet service provider can be difficult. Find out if the ISP offers customer support in the evenings and on weekends as well as during business hours.

Publish Web Pages

You can create Web pages to share business or personal information with people around the world. Look for a service provider that will publish Web pages you create. Many ISPs let you publish and maintain Web pages for free.

Type of Connection

There are three ways you can connect to an Internet service provider.

A Point-to-Point Protocol (PPP) connection is the most popular and most reliable way to connect to a provider using a modem. Serial Line Internet Protocol (SLIP) and Compressed SLIP (CSLIP) are older and less reliable ways to connect to a provider.

GETTING CONNECTED

COMMERCIAL ONLINE SERVICE

A commercial online service is a company that offers a vast amount of information and access to the Internet for a fee.

Commercial Online Service

Cost

Most commercial online services let you try their service free of charge for a limited time. After the trial period, most online services offer a certain number of hours per day or month for a set fee.

If you exceed the total number of hours, you are usually charged for every extra hour you use the online service.

Most online services do not charge a fee for setting up your connection to the Internet.

POPULAR COMMERCIAL ONLINE SERVICES

Popular online services include America Online, CompuServe and The Microsoft Network.

America Online

CompuServe

The Microsoft Network

COMMERCIAL ONLINE SERVICE FEATURES

Information

An online service offers information such as daily news, stock quotes, weather reports, encyclopedias, dictionaries and magazines. This information is well-organized and easy to find, unlike information on the Internet.

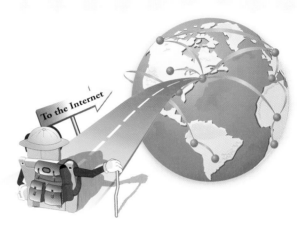

Internet Access

All the major online services offer access to the Internet.

Getting Help

Setting up a connection to an online service is relatively easy. Online services usually provide good customer support for questions you may have.

Chat

Chatting is a very popular feature of online services. You can instantly communicate with other people connected to the service by simply typing back and forth. Chatting is a great way to meet people and exchange ideas.

When you chat, the text you type immediately appears on the screen of each person involved in the conversation.

SERVICE PROVIDER LISTING

There are service providers all over the world that can give you access to the Internet. You can find service providers in telephone books, local newspapers and magazines.

Many providers service Internet users both in Canada and the United States.

America Online®
U.S.A.: 1-800-827-6364
CDN: 1-888-265-4357

CompuServe
1-800-848-8990

Delphi
1-800-695-4005

Microsoft Network
1-800-386-5550

EarthLink Network
1-800-395-8425

Genie
1-800-638-9636

NETCOM
1-800-353-6600

Prodigy
1-800-PRODIGY

UNITED STATES

Atlanta, Georgia
Intergate (770) 429-9599
Epoch Networks (404) 898-2500

Chicago, Illinois
NetWave (312) 335-8038
Tezcat Communications (312) 850-0181

Houston, Texas
Digital Mainstream (713) 364-1819
NetTap (713) 482-3903

Los Angeles, California
LA Internet (213) 932-1999
LightSide (818) 858-9261

Miami, Florida
CyberGate (954) 428-4283
Internet World Information Network (305) 535-3090

New York City, New York
Interport (212) 989-1128
New York Connect.Net (212) 293-2620

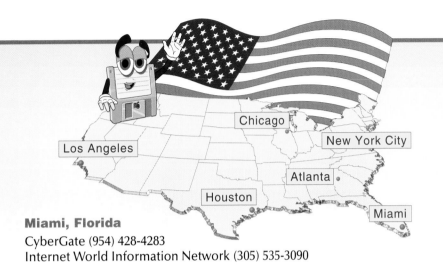

INTERNATIONAL

Australia
Geko (02) 9439.1999
Magnadata (02) 9272.9600

Japan
Global Online Japan (03) 5330.9380
Twics Internet (03) 3351.5977

Canada
Internet Direct (416) 233-7150
Pro.NET (604) 688-9282
Sympatico 1-800-773-2121

South Africa
Internet Africa (21) 689.6242
Internet Solutions (11) 447.5566

Ireland
EU Net Ireland (16) 790832
Ireland Online (01) 855.1739

United Kingdom
Atlas Internet (0171) 312.0400
Demon Systems (0181) 349.0063

CHAPTER 2

THE WORLD WIDE WEB

What is the World Wide Web? This chapter introduces you to the Web and what it has to offer. You will learn about browsers, multimedia, shopping and much more.

The World Wide Web is part of the Internet. The Web consists of a huge collection of documents stored on computers around the world.

The World Wide Web is also called the Web, WWW or W3.

Web Page

A Web page is a document on the Web. Web pages can include text, pictures, sound and video.

Web Server

A Web server is a computer connected to the Internet that makes Web pages available to the world.

Web Site

A Web site is a collection of Web pages maintained by a college, university, government agency, company or individual.

URL

Each Web page has a unique address, called the Uniform Resource Locator (URL). You can instantly display any Web page if you know its URL.

■ All Web page URLs start with http (HyperText Transfer Protocol).

HYPERTEXT

Web pages are hypertext documents. A hypertext document contains highlighted text that connects to other pages on the Web. You can select highlighted text on a Web page to display a page located on the same computer or a computer across the city, country or world.

Highlighted text allows you to easily navigate through a vast amount of information by jumping from one Web page to another.

WEB BROWSERS

A Web browser is a program that lets you view and explore information on the World Wide Web.

Netscape Navigator

Netscape Navigator is currently the most popular Web browser used to view Web pages. Navigator is available for computers running many different operating systems, including OS/2, Macintosh, Windows and Unix. Navigator is also available in over 10 different languages.

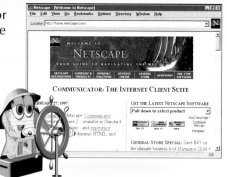

You can get Netscape Navigator at the following Web site:

http://home.netscape.com

Microsoft Internet Explorer

Microsoft Internet Explorer is a newer Web browser that is quickly becoming one of the most popular Web browsers. Internet Explorer was created by the same company that created the Windows operating systems. This means that the look and feel of Internet Explorer is similar to the look and feel of other Windows programs.

You can get Internet Explorer free of charge at the following Web site:

http://www.microsoft.com/ie

Beta Versions

A beta version of a Web browser is an early version of the program that is not quite ready for sale. Many companies let people use and test the beta versions of their Web browsers before releasing the official versions. Beta versions of Web browsers sometimes contain errors.

Bookmarks

Most Web browsers have a feature called bookmarks or favorites. This feature lets you store the addresses of Web pages you frequently visit. Bookmarks save you from having to remember and constantly retype your favorite Web page addresses.

History List

When you are browsing through pages on the World Wide Web, it can be difficult to keep track of the locations of pages you have visited. Most Web browsers include a history list that allows you to quickly return to any Web page you have recently visited.

Netscape Navigator needs special programs, called plug-ins, to display or play certain types of files on the Web. A plug-in performs tasks Navigator cannot perform on its own.

Error Messages

An error message appears when Navigator cannot display or play a file you selected. You must get the appropriate plug-in before you can work with the file.

Getting Plug-Ins

If you want to display or play a file Navigator cannot work with, you can download (copy) the appropriate plug-in from the Web. Most plug-ins are offered free of charge. After you download a plug-in, the program will work with Navigator to display or play the file.

You can find a list of many popular plug-ins at the following Web site:

http://www.netscape.com/comprod/upgrades/index.html

POPULAR PLUG-INS

Acrobat Reader

Acrobat Reader lets you view and print Portable Document Format (PDF) files. Acrobat Reader lets you see on screen how your document will look when printed.

You can get Acrobat Reader at the following Web site:

http://www.adobe.com

Crescendo

Crescendo lets you listen to background music while viewing text and images on a Web page. When you visit a Web page that uses Crescendo, the music begins to play almost immediately.

You can get Crescendo at the following Web site:

http://www.liveupdate.com/midi.html

QuickTime

QuickTime lets you view and listen to multimedia on any type of computer, such as a PC or a Macintosh.

You can get QuickTime at the following Web site:

http://quicktime.apple.com

Shockwave

Shockwave lets you view video and animation while listening to music and sound effects. Shockwave is often used for games and interactive presentations.

You can get Shockwave at the following Web site:

http://www.macromedia.com

Frames

Some Web pages divide information into rectangular sections, called frames. Each frame displays a different Web page.

Forms

Some Web pages include forms that let you enter information. The information you type into a form travels across the Internet to the computer that maintains the page. Many companies use forms to allow readers to express their opinions, ask questions or order goods and services.

Tables

Some Web pages display information in tables. A table organizes information into an easy-to-follow, attractive format. Tables in Web pages often display lists of information, such as financial data, telephone directories and price lists. Tables can include images as well as text.

You can buy products and services on the Web without ever leaving your desk.

There are thousands of products you can buy on the Web, such as clothing, flowers, office supplies and computer programs.

The Web also offers a range of services, such as banking and financial or real estate advice.

Companies

Thousands of companies have Web sites where you can get product information and buy products and services online.

You can view a list of companies on the Web at the following site:

http://www.cio.com/central/businesses.html

Shopping Malls

There are shopping malls on the Web where you can view and buy products and services offered by many different companies.

You can view a list of shopping malls on the Web at the following site:

http://nsns.com/MouseTracks/HallofMalls.html

Many Web pages require you to enter confidential information about yourself to use the services they offer. There are secure pages on the Web that will protect confidential information sent over the Internet.

When you send information over the Internet, the information may pass through many computers before reaching its destination.

If you are not connected to a secure Web page, people may be able to view the information you send.

Secure Web Pages

Secure Web pages work with Web browsers that support security features to create an almost unbreakable security system. When you connect to a secure Web page, other people on the Internet cannot view the information you transfer.

Visit Secure Web Pages

When a reader visits a secure Web page, the Web browser will usually display a solid key or a lock at the bottom corner of the screen. This indicates that the Web page is secure.

Microsoft Internet Explorer   Netscape Navigator

REASONS FOR USING SECURITY

Credit Cards

Many people feel it is unsafe to transmit credit card numbers over the Internet. In fact, sending a credit card number over a secure connection can be safer than giving the number to an unknown person over the phone or by fax.

Companies

Some people work at home and use the Internet to connect to computers at the office. Secure Web pages allow employees to access confidential information that companies would not make available over connections that are not secure.

Banking

Many banks allow you to access your banking information over the Web. You can pay bills, transfer money between accounts and even apply for a loan.

Banking information is one of the most confidential types of information. Banks use secure Web pages to keep this information private.

A Web page can contain text, images, sound, video and animation.

Multimedia is an effective way of attracting attention to information on a Web page. Many companies that advertise on the Web use a combination of text, images, sound and video or animation to sell their products and services.

Transfer Time

Some files take a while to transfer to your computer. A Web page usually shows you the size of a file to give you an indication of how long the file will take to transfer.

Use this chart as a guide to determine how long a file will take to transfer to your computer.

	File Size		Time
Bytes	Kilobytes (KB)	Megabytes (MB)	(estimated)
10,000,000	10,000	10	1 hour
5,000,000	5,000	5	30 minutes
2,500,000	2,500	2.5	15 minutes

This chart is based on transferring files with a 28,800 bps modem. A modem with a speed of 14,400 bps or lower will transfer files more slowly than shown in the chart.

Text

You can view documents on the Web such as newspapers, magazines, plays, famous speeches and television show transcripts.

Text transfers quickly to your computer, so you do not have to wait long to read text on a Web page.

Images

You can view images on the Web such as album covers, pictures of celebrities and famous paintings.

Sound

You can hear sound on the Web such as TV theme songs, movie soundtracks, sound effects and historical speeches.

You need a sound card and speakers to hear sound on the Web.

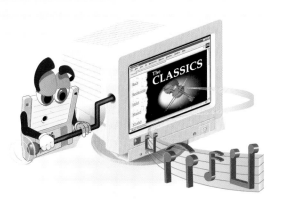

Video and Animation

You can view video and animation on the Web such as movie clips, cartoons and interviews with celebrities.

Video and animation files often take a while to transfer to your computer.

RealAudio is a program that lets you listen to sound such as live radio shows, music or interviews on the World Wide Web.

You can get the RealAudio sound player at the following Web site:

http://www.realaudio.com

Streaming Audio

RealAudio uses a system called streaming audio to transfer sound to your computer. Other programs that play sound must transfer the entire sound file to your computer before you can listen to the sound. With streaming audio, you can listen to the sound while the file is transferring.

RealAudio Sites

There are many new RealAudio Web sites created every week.

You can find examples of RealAudio sound at the following locations:

WGRR 103.5 Cincinnati

http://www.wgrr1035.com/cgi-bin/rightnow/rightnow

National Museum of American Art

http://www.nmaa.si.edu/masterdir/pagesub/whatnew.html

Microsoft Music Central

http://MusicCentral.msn.com/Default.asp

You can get a RealVideo player at the following Web site:

http://www.realaudio.com

Streaming Video

RealVideo uses a system called streaming video to transfer information from a content provider to a RealVideo player on your computer. Streaming video lets the RealVideo player start displaying the video information while the file is still transferring to your computer. Other programs require the entire video file to transfer before you can watch the video.

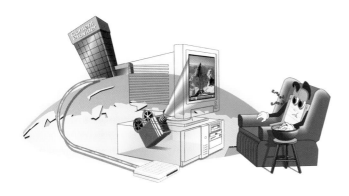

Content

Content for RealVideo is available from a varied range of services. Companies that supply RealVideo information on the Internet are known as RealVideo content providers. Many types of RealVideo information are available, such as news, sports and business highlights. You can visit some RealVideo content providers on the World Wide Web at this site:

http://www.timecast.com/videoguide.html

> Java is a programming language that allows you to create animated and interactive Web pages.

A Java program used in a Web page is called a Java applet.

How Java Works

Java applets are stored on a Web server. When a reader displays a Web page containing a Java applet, the applet transfers from the Web server to the reader's computer and then runs. Some Java applets take a long time to transfer.

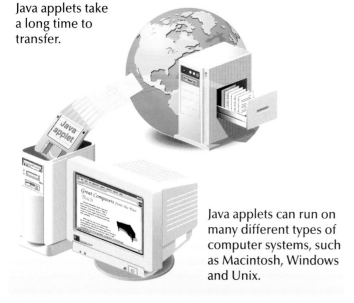

Java applets can run on many different types of computer systems, such as Macintosh, Windows and Unix.

Web Browsers

Before viewing a Java applet on a Web page, a reader must have a Web browser that can run Java applets. Most new Web browsers can run Java applets.

REASONS FOR USING JAVA

Web Page Enhancements

Most people use Java applets to enhance their Web pages. Many applets are used to display moving text or simple animation.

You can view a collection of Java applets at the following Web site:

http://www.gamelan.com

Interactive Web Pages

People often include Java applets in their Web pages to allow readers to interact with each other on the Web. Some Java applets allow readers to play games or chat with other people.

Programs

Java is also used to write complex programs such as word processing, spreadsheet and drawing programs. These types of Java applets are very large. Most people do not include this type of Java applet in their Web pages because the applets take too long to transfer.

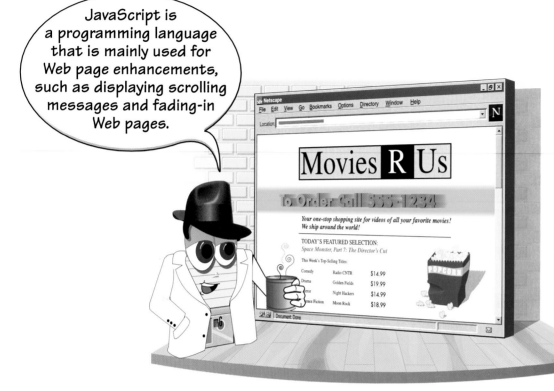

JavaScript is a programming language that is mainly used for Web page enhancements, such as displaying scrolling messages and fading-in Web pages.

Although the names are similar, JavaScript and Java have very little in common. JavaScript is easier to learn than Java.

How JavaScript Works

JavaScript instructions are placed in the HTML document. You can view examples of JavaScript at the following Web site:

http://www.gamelan.com

Web Browsers

Before viewing JavaScript on a Web page, a reader must have a Web browser that can run JavaScript instructions. Most new Web browsers can run JavaScript.

ActiveX is a newer technology developed by Microsoft to help you improve your Web pages.

Reasons for Using ActiveX

ActiveX is commonly used in Web pages to add pop-up menus that instantly display a list of options.

ActiveX is also used to include animated images and information from popular programs, such as Microsoft Word or Microsoft Excel, in Web pages.

Web Browsers

Before viewing a Web page that includes ActiveX features, a reader must have a Web browser that supports ActiveX. Microsoft Internet Explorer has built-in support for ActiveX.

Some Web browsers, including Netscape Navigator, currently do not have built-in support. Readers who want to use ActiveX with Navigator can get a special program at the following Web site:

http://www.ncompasslabs.com

VRML

Virtual Reality Modeling Language (VRML) allows you to view three-dimensional objects and environments, called VRML worlds in Web pages.

VRML Viewers

A VRML viewer lets you use a mouse or keyboard to move through three-dimensional areas or walk around objects in a VRML world. To display a VRML world, a Web browser must support VRML. Most new browsers support VRML.

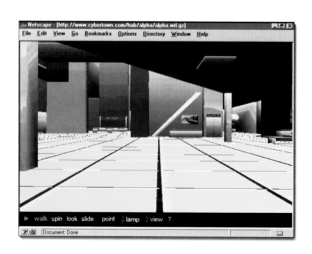

Virtual Objects

You can view a virtual object from any angle. You can walk around a virtual object and move closer or farther away from the object.

A virtual object can be a car, truck, plane, lamp or any other item in the real world.

REASONS FOR USING VRML

Entertainment

VRML is used to create three-dimensional towns, movies and games. When playing a VRML game, you can compete against other people on the Web.

You can find entertaining VRML worlds at the following Web sites:

http://www.cybertown.com/3dvd.html

http://www.virtualvegas.com

Product Demonstrations

Companies often use VRML to show their products. You can walk around products and view them from any angle. This gives you control that you do not have when viewing television or magazine advertisements.

Two companies that allow you to view their products using VRML are at the following Web sites:

http://www.netvision.net.il/~teldor/vrml.html

http://www.asia-online.com.sg/perfection/es300/features.html

Training

In the future, there will be VRML worlds that allow people to use the Internet to train at home instead of going to a classroom.

Companies will also create VRML worlds to provide instruction on tasks such as servicing electronic products or repairing cars.

SEARCH THE WEB

> There are many free services you can use to find information on the Web. These services are called search tools.

A search tool catalogs Web pages to make them easier to find. Some search tools record every word on a Web page, while others only record the name of each page.

You can see a list of various search tools at the following Web sites:

http://www.search.com/alpha.html

http://home.netscape.com/home/internet-search.html

HOW SEARCH TOOLS FIND WEB PAGES

There are two ways a search tool finds pages on the Web.

Since hundreds of new pages are created each day, it is impossible for a search tool to catalog every new page on the Web.

Spiders
Most search tools have automated robots, called spiders, that travel around the Web looking for new pages.

Submissions
People submit information about pages they have created.

SEARCH METHODS

There are two ways a search tool can help you find information on the Web.

Search by Category

You can browse through categories such as arts, science and sports to find information that interests you.

Select a category of interest and a list of subcategories appears.

Continue to select subcategories until you find a page that interests you.

Search by Topic

You can search for a specific topic that interests you.

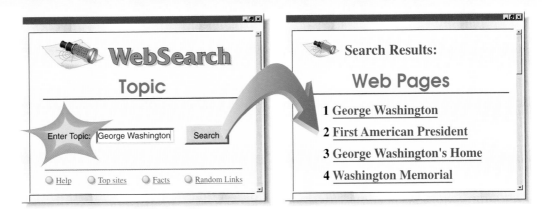

Type in a topic of interest.

When the search is complete, a list of pages containing the topic you specified appears.

SEARCH THE WEB

Alta Vista

Alta Vista lets you search for a specific topic of interest. You can choose to search Web pages or Usenet, a part of the Internet that contains discussion groups, called newsgroups.

You can access Alta Vista at the following Web site:

http://altavista.digital.com

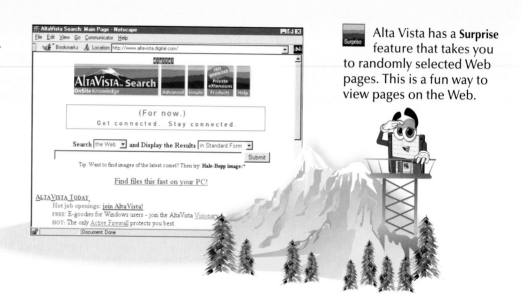

Alta Vista has a **Surprise** feature that takes you to randomly selected Web pages. This is a fun way to view pages on the Web.

Infoseek

Infoseek lets you search for a specific topic of interest or browse through categories, such as education or travel.

You can choose to search Web pages, e-mail addresses or Usenet, a part of the Internet that contains discussion groups, called newsgroups.

You can access Infoseek at the following Web site:

http://www.infoseek.com

Infoseek has an **Infoseek Investor** feature that gives you quick access to stock quotes and information about thousands of U.S. companies.

Lycos

Lycos lets you search for a specific topic of interest or browse through categories, such as computers or sports.

You can access Lycos at the following Web site:

http://www.lycos.com

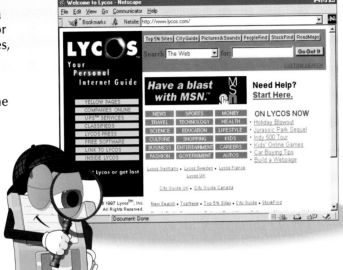

POINT Lycos offers a connection to **Point**, a search tool that keeps track of the best pages on the Web. You can browse through categories or type in a topic and Point will display the top-ranked pages matching your request.

Yahoo

Yahoo lets you search for a specific topic of interest or browse through categories, such as arts or science.

You can access Yahoo at the following Web site:

http://www.yahoo.com

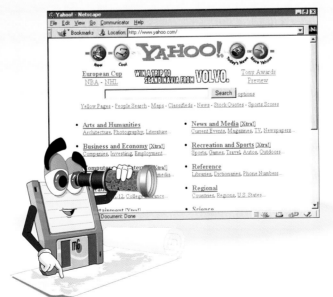

Yahoo has a **Cool** feature that takes you to Web pages Yahoo considers innovative and interesting.

Yahoo also has a **Today's News** feature that gives you up-to-date news for various categories such as entertainment, politics and sports.

CREATE WEB PAGES

> You can create and publish Web pages to share information with people around the world.

WHY PUBLISH?

Individuals publish on the Web to share their favorite pictures, hobbies and interests.

Companies publish on the Web to promote their businesses, advertise products and publicize job openings.

WEB PAGE ORGANIZATION

Home Page

A home page provides a general introduction to your Web pages. A home page often includes a table of contents that describes all of your Web pages.

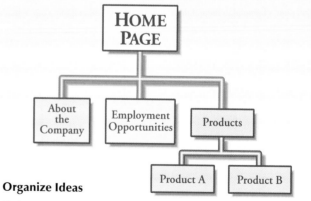

Organize Ideas

Before you start creating Web pages, decide what ideas you will discuss and how the ideas relate to one another. Break up your information so you discuss only one major idea on each page. You may find it helpful to first sketch the design of your pages on paper.

HTML

HyperText Markup Language (HTML) is a computer language used to create Web pages.

An HTML document has the extension .html or .htm (example: index.html).

Text Editors and Word Processors

You can create HTML documents using a text editor or word processor.

You enter HTML text commands, called tags, to define how text and graphics will appear on a page. Tags usually work in pairs and affect the text between the tags. For example, the tags <B>dog</B> will make the text "dog" appear in **bold**.

HTML Editors

You can also create HTML documents using HTML editors, such as Microsoft FrontPage or Netscape Gold.

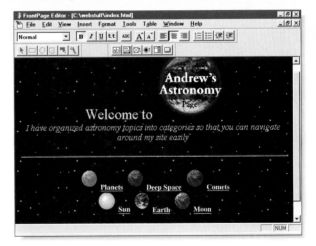

HTML editors make it easier to create Web pages because they enter tags for you. This means you do not need to know the HTML computer language to create Web pages.

IMAGES

You can add images to your Web pages to make the pages more attractive.

Avoid placing a large number of images on your Web pages. Images increase the time it takes for pages to appear on the screen.

Create Images

You can use a graphics program, such as Adobe Photoshop or Corel PHOTO-PAINT, to create images you can add to Web pages.

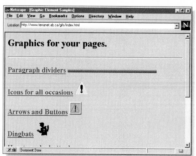

Copy Images

There are places on the Internet that offer images you can use on your Web pages. Make sure you have permission to use any images you copy from the Internet.

You can also buy a collection of ready-made images, called clip art, at most computer stores.

Scan Images

You can use a scanner to scan pictures, drawings and logos into a computer. You can then use the scanned images on your Web pages.

LINKS

> You can add links to your Web pages.

Links allow readers to select highlighted text or images to display other, related pages on the Web.

Where to Link

You can place links on your Web pages that connect to other pages you have created. This helps readers flip through your Web pages.

You can also place links on your Web pages that connect to pages maintained by other organizations. This gives readers instant access to related information.

Be Descriptive

Make sure you describe linked pages accurately so readers will know if they want to select a link. Telling readers to "click here" is not very informative.

Check Links

Web page addresses sometimes change. You should regularly check all the links on your Web pages to make sure the addresses are still correct.

CREATE WEB PAGES

> Once you have created your Web pages, you need to publish the pages so people around the world can view them.

You publish Web pages by transferring the pages to a Web server. A Web server is a computer connected to the Internet that makes your pages available to the world.

Where to Publish Web Pages

The service that connects you to the Internet may offer space on its Web server where you can store your Web pages free of charge. The service may limit the amount of space you can use.

Maintain Web Pages

After you publish Web pages, make sure you keep the information on the pages up-to-date. Incorporate feedback you receive from readers and try to improve the content and design of the pages whenever possible.

PUBLICIZE WEB PAGES

Search Tools

You can use the **Submit It!** Web site to announce your Web pages. The **Submit It!** site sends information about your Web pages to many different search tools. Search tools help people find pages on the Web. You can access **Submit It!** at the following Web site:

http://www.submit-it.com/index.html

Exchange Links

If another page on the Web discusses related ideas, ask if they will place a link to your page if you do the same.

Off the Internet

You can publicize your Web page address on business cards and company letterhead. Companies often include Web page addresses in television, radio, newspaper and magazine advertisements.

Web Pages

Many companies set aside areas on their Web pages for advertisements. For a fee, you can use these areas to advertise your Web pages.

An Internet television terminal is an electronic device that plugs into your television, allowing you to explore certain parts of the Internet.

Internet television terminals are also known as set top boxes. You can find out more about Internet television terminals from WebTV by calling 1-800-GOWEBTV or by checking out the following Web site:

http://www.webtv.net

Software

The software used to access the Internet is built into the Internet television terminal. Each terminal has applications that allow you to browse the World Wide Web and use e-mail. The applications used in the terminal can often be updated using the Internet.

Modem

Internet television terminals have a built-in modem. Before you can use the terminal, you have to connect it to a phone line. When you use the Internet with the terminal, it automatically dials a number and connects you to the Internet service provider. Most terminals have a modem with a speed of 33.6 Kb/s.

Services

The main purpose of Internet television terminals is to allow people to browse the World Wide Web. All Internet television terminals also allow you to send and receive e-mail messages.

Most terminals allow individual family members to have their own e-mail addresses.

Display

Internet television terminals connect to a television and use the television to display images.

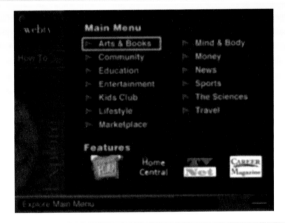

Some Web pages that are displayed on the television screen may not be as sharp looking as when viewed on a computer monitor, which offers higher resolutions and more colors than most televisions.

Remote Control

Most Internet television terminals come equipped with a remote control. You can use the remote control instead of a mouse while browsing the World Wide Web. Terminals can also be used with a keyboard, which makes it easy to enter text.

If you plan to send many e-mail messages, you should use a keyboard.

CHAPTER 3

ELECTRONIC MAIL

What is electronic mail? Find out in this chapter how the Internet's most popular feature lets you communicate with people around the world.

You can exchange electronic mail (e-mail) with people around the world.

E-mail provides a fast, economical and convenient way to send messages to family, friends and colleagues.

SPEED

E-mail is much faster than old-fashioned mail, called "snail mail." An e-mail message can travel around the world in minutes.

COST

Once you pay a service provider for a connection to the Internet, there is no charge for sending and receiving e-mail. You do not have to pay extra even if you send a long message or the message travels around the world.

Exchanging e-mail can save you money on long-distance calls. The next time you are about to pick up the telephone, consider sending an e-mail message instead.

E-MAIL PROGRAMS

An *e-mail program* lets you send, receive and manage your e-mail messages.

POPULAR E-MAIL PROGRAMS

Popular e-mail programs include Eudora Light and Netscape Mail.

EUDORA LIGHT

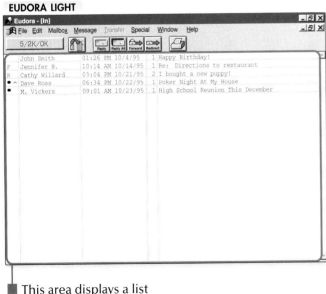

NETSCAPE MAIL

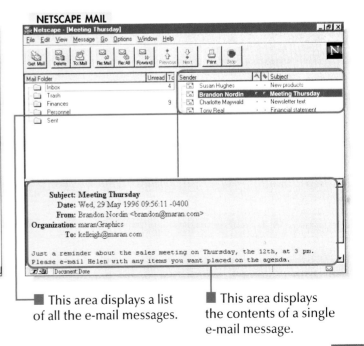

■ This area displays a list of all the e-mail messages.

■ This area displays a list of all the e-mail messages.

■ This area displays the contents of a single e-mail message.

You can send a message to anyone around the world if you know the person's e-mail address.

mvickers@ipdirect.com

An e-mail address defines the location of an individual's mailbox on the Internet.

PARTS OF AN E-MAIL ADDRESS

An e-mail address consists of two parts separated by the @ (at) symbol. An e-mail address cannot contain spaces.

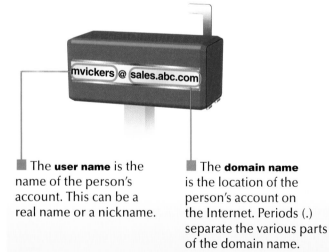

mvickers @ sales.abc.com

■ The **user name** is the name of the person's account. This can be a real name or a nickname.

■ The **domain name** is the location of the person's account on the Internet. Periods (.) separate the various parts of the domain name.

FAMOUS E-MAIL ADDRESSES

FAMOUS

NAME	ADDRESS
Bill Gates	billg@microsoft.com
Brad Pitt	ciaobox@msn.com
Madonna	Madonna@wbr.com
U.S. President	president@whitehouse.gov
Tom Brokaw	nightly@nbc.com
Tom Clancy	tomclancy@aol.com

ORGANIZATION OR COUNTRY

The last few characters in an e-mail address usually indicate the type of organization or country to which the person belongs.

ORGANIZATION

com	commercial
edu	education
gov	government
mil	military
net	network
org	organization (often non-profit)

COUNTRY

au	Australia
ca	Canada
it	Italy
jp	Japan
uk	United Kingdom

PASSPORT

FIND E-MAIL ADDRESSES

There is no central listing of e-mail addresses. The best way to find the e-mail addresses of friends or colleagues is to phone them and ask.

There are many places on the Web that help you search for e-mail addresses free of charge. The following Web site allows you to search for e-mail addresses:

http://www.four11.com

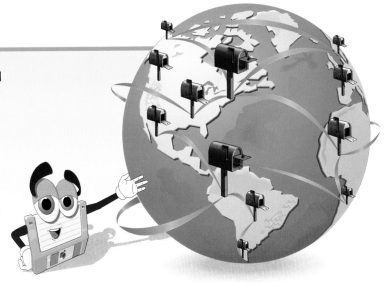

Writing Style

Make sure every message you send is clear, concise and contains no spelling or grammar errors. Also make sure the message will not be misinterpreted. For example, the reader may not realize a statement is meant to be sarcastic.

Smileys

You can use special characters, called smileys or emoticons, to express emotions in messages. The characters resemble human faces if you turn them sideways.

SMILEYS

Gesture	Characters
Cry	:'-(
Frown	:-(
Indifferent	:-I
Laugh	:-D
Smile	:-)
Surprise	:-0
Wink	;-)

Abbreviations

Abbreviations are commonly used in messages to save time typing.

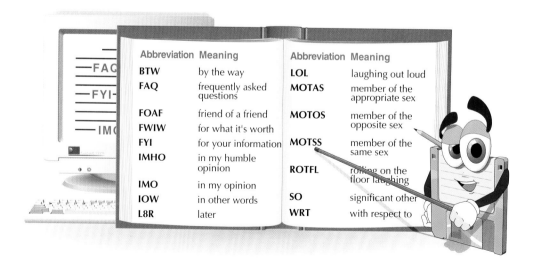

Abbreviation	Meaning
BTW	by the way
FAQ	frequently asked questions
FOAF	friend of a friend
FWIW	for what it's worth
FYI	for your information
IMHO	in my humble opinion
IMO	in my opinion
IOW	in other words
L8R	later

Abbreviation	Meaning
LOL	laughing out loud
MOTAS	member of the appropriate sex
MOTOS	member of the opposite sex
MOTSS	member of the same sex
ROTFL	rolling on the floor laughing
SO	significant other
WRT	with respect to

Shouting

A MESSAGE WRITTEN IN CAPITAL LETTERS IS ANNOYING AND HARD TO READ. THIS IS CALLED SHOUTING.

Always use upper and lower case letters when typing messages.

Flame

A flame is an angry or insulting message directed at one person. A flame war is an argument that continues for a while.

Avoid starting or participating in flame wars.

Signature

You can have an e-mail program add information about yourself to the end of every message you send. This prevents you from having to type the same information over and over again.

A signature can include your name, e-mail address, occupation or favorite quotation. You can also use plain characters to display simple pictures. Do not create a signature that is more than four lines long.

From:
Address of the
person sending
the message.

From:	mary@sales.abc.com
To:	john@sales.abc.com
Subject:	Sales Awards
Cc:	sarah@sales.abc.com
Bcc:	karen@abc.com

Congratulations on your achievement!
I'm looking forward to seeing you at the
awards ceremony!

To:
Address of the person
receiving the message.

Subject:
Identifies the contents of
the message. Make sure
your subject is informative.
Do not use subjects such
as "For your information"
or "Read this now."

Cc:
Stands for "carbon copy." A
carbon copy is an exact copy
of a message. You can send a
carbon copy of a message to
a person who is not directly
involved, but would be
interested in the message.

Bcc:
Stands for "blind carbon
copy." This lets you send
the same message to
several people without
them knowing that others
have also received the
same message.

Many e-mail programs use Multipurpose Internet Mail Extensions (MIME) to attach files to messages.

To view an attached file, the computer receiving the message must be able to understand MIME. The computer must also have a program that can view or play the file.

COMPRESS ATTACHED FILES

When you want to attach a large file to an e-mail message, you can save time and money by compressing the file. Compressing a file shrinks the file to a smaller size. This allows the file to transfer more quickly over the Internet.

You can also use a compression program to combine numerous files into a single file. This means you do not need to attach each file individually to an e-mail message.

The person receiving a compressed file must use a decompression program to expand the file to its original form.

If you want to practice sending a message, send a message to yourself.

When you send a message, do not assume the person will read the message right away. Some people may not regularly check their messages.

COMPOSE OFFLINE

You can write e-mail messages when you are not connected to the Internet (offline). When you finish writing all your messages, you can connect and send the messages all at once. This saves you money since you do not have to pay for the time you spend composing messages.

USE THE ADDRESS BOOK

An e-mail program provides an address book where you can store the addresses of people you frequently send messages to. An address book saves you from having to type the same addresses over and over again.

SEND PRIVATE MESSAGES

There are ways to send messages privately over the Internet. This protects messages from crackers who illegally break into computer systems for fun or to steal information.

BOUNCED MESSAGES

A bounced message is a message that returns to you because it cannot reach its destination. A message usually bounces because of typing mistakes in the e-mail address. Before sending a message, double-check the e-mail address.

Receive Messages

Your Internet access provider stores messages you receive in a mailbox for you. When you check for new messages, you are checking your mailbox on the access provider's computer.

Check for new messages on a regular basis. If your mailbox gets too full, your access provider may delete some of your messages.

You can use most computers with a modem to connect to your access provider and retrieve messages. This allows you to check your messages while traveling.

Automatically Check for Messages

Most e-mail programs automatically check for new e-mail messages. You can specify how often you want the program to check for new messages.

You should have the e-mail program check for messages approximately every 30 minutes. If your e-mail program is constantly checking for new messages, it can slow down the performance of other tasks, such as browsing the Web.

Reply to a Message

You can reply to a message to answer a question, express an opinion or supply additional information.

When you reply to a message, make sure you include part of the original message. This is called quoting. Quoting helps the reader identify which message you are replying to. To save the reader time, make sure you delete all parts of the original message that do not directly relate to your reply.

Forward a Message

After reading a message, you can add comments and then send the message to a friend or colleague.

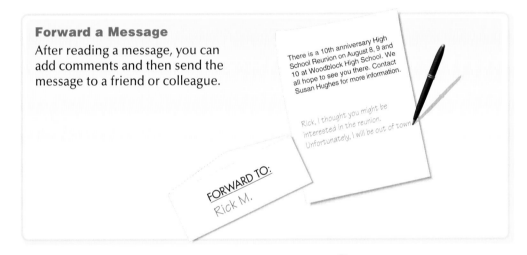

Print a Message

You can print a message to produce a paper copy.

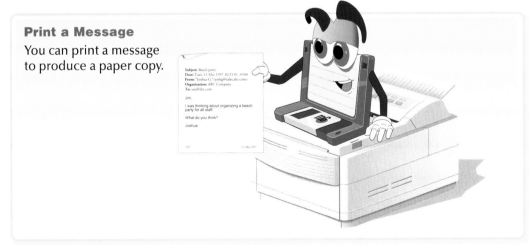

E-MAIL SECURITY

When you use PGP to make an e-mail message private, only the person you send the message to can read the message.

You can get PGP at the following Web site:

http://thegate.gamers.org/~tony/pgp.html

PGP Keys

PGP uses two codes, called keys, to keep your messages confidential. The two keys work together to make sure you are the only person who can read confidential messages you receive.

If you want a friend or colleague to send you a confidential message, you must give them your **public key** to encode the message for you. You can give people your public key by e-mail or over the telephone.

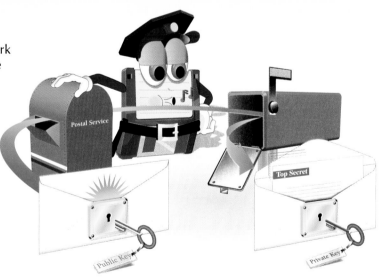

When you receive a confidential message, you use your **private key** to decode the message. You must always keep your private key secret.

72

PGP Versions

PGP is the most secure privacy program available on the Internet. There are currently two versions of PGP available. This is because the PGP code is so difficult to crack that the U.S. government has declared the program a weapon.

The most secure version can only be used in the United States and Canada. The other version of the program can be used in the rest of the world.

PGP Helper Programs

Some e-mail programs have built-in features that make the programs easier to use with PGP. You can also find many helper programs on the Internet that make PGP easier to use. PGP helper programs are available for most computer operating systems including Windows, Macintosh and Unix.

You can find PGP helper programs at the following Web sites:

http://www.primenet.com/~shauert/pgpwins.htm

http://web.mit.edu/network/pgp.html

Some people enjoy using e-mail to play pranks or jokes on other people on the Internet. An e-mail prank begins when someone sends an e-mail message containing an untrue rumor.

Elvis will be in NYC today!

The ability to send e-mail messages anonymously on the Internet makes it easy for anyone to spread false stories.

POPULAR E-MAIL PRANKS

Modem Tax

This prank claims that a certain politician is about to introduce a new law requiring people who use modems to pay a special tax, called a modem tax. The e-mail message asks readers to contact their local politicians to protest this new tax.

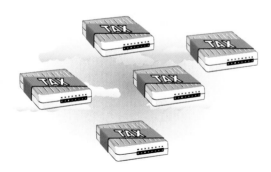

Good Times Virus

A computer virus is a program that can damage data stored on a computer. The good times virus prank claims that an e-mail message containing a virus is being circulated on the Internet. Readers are warned the virus will infect their computers when they read the message. The good times virus has never existed, but these warnings continue to circulate.

Postcard Collection

Several years ago in England, a boy who was sick requested that people send him postcards so he could get into the Guinness Book of Records for the largest collection of postcards. His wish was fulfilled, but some people still falsely circulate the story about the boy to try and fool others into sending postcards.

Cookie Recipe

This prank is spread by someone claiming they bought a cookie recipe from a prestigious restaurant for what they thought was $2.50. But when they paid, the price turned out to be $250. To get even with the restaurant, the person is distributing the recipe for free on the Internet.

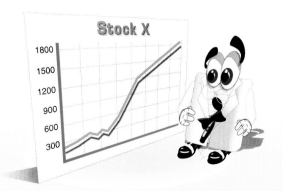

Hot Stocks

Many false rumors pass over the Internet about insider tips, or privileged information, about supposedly smart investments. Making investments based on what you read on the Internet is not wise because many people provide tips for their own benefit. Never send money to anyone who promises high rates of return on investments.

CHAPTER 4

MAILING LISTS

Do you want to learn about mailing lists? This chapter introduces you to mailing lists and provides a number of interesting mailing lists you can join.

Mailing List

A mailing list is a discussion group that uses e-mail to communicate.

There are thousands of mailing lists that cover a wide variety of topics, from aromatherapy to ZZ Top. New mailing lists are created every week.

How Mailing Lists Work

When a mailing list receives a message, a copy of the message goes to everyone on the mailing list.

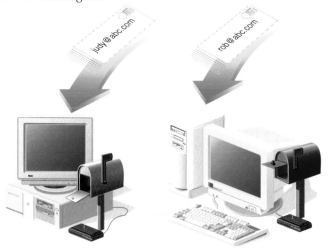

Most mailing lists let you send and receive messages. Some mailing lists only let you receive messages.

Find Mailing Lists

You can find an index of mailing lists at the following Web site:

http://www.neosoft.com/internet/paml

You can search for mailing lists that discuss a specific topic at the following Web site:

http://www.liszt.com

Cost

You can join most mailing lists free of charge. Mailing lists that charge people to join are usually used for distributing newsletters and electronic news such as stock market figures.

Start a Mailing List

You can easily start your own mailing list. If only a few people will be using the list, you can run the list with a regular e-mail program on your own computer. Most Internet access providers have programs dedicated to running large mailing lists for their customers. Running your own mailing list can be very time-consuming.

Get Information

Before you join a mailing list, try to get as much information as possible about the list. Most mailing lists have their own rules and regulations. Mailing lists often provide an e-mail address where you can send a message to request information about the list.

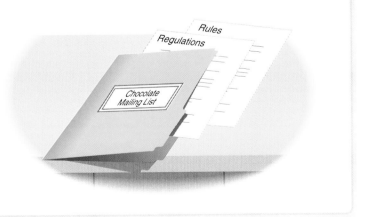

Just as you would subscribe to a newspaper or magazine, you can subscribe to a mailing list that interests you.

Subscribing adds your e-mail address to the mailing list.

Unsubscribe

If you no longer want to receive messages from a mailing list, you can unsubscribe from the mailing list at any time. Unsubscribing removes your e-mail address from the mailing list.

MAILING LIST ADDRESSES

Each mailing list has two addresses. Make sure you send your messages to the appropriate address.

Mailing List Address

The mailing list address receives messages intended for the entire mailing list. This is the address you use to send messages you want all the people on the list to receive. Do not send subscription or unsubscription requests to the mailing list address.

Administrative Address

The administrative address receives messages dealing with administrative issues. This is the address you use to subscribe to or unsubscribe from a mailing list.

Welcome Message

When you subscribe to a mailing list, you will receive a welcome message to confirm that your e-mail address has been added to the list. This message will also explain any rules the mailing list has about sending messages to the list.

Check for Messages

After you subscribe to a mailing list, make sure you check your mailbox frequently. You can receive dozens of messages in a short period of time.

Digests

If you receive a lot of messages from a mailing list, find out if the list is available as a digest. A digest groups individual messages together and sends them to you as one message.

Vacations

When you go on vacation, make sure you temporarily unsubscribe from all your mailing lists. This will prevent your mailbox from overflowing with messages.

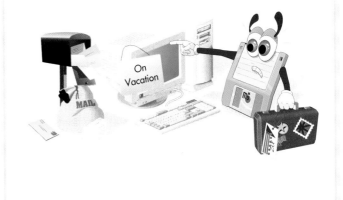

Manually Maintained Lists

A person manages a manually maintained mailing list.

A manually maintained list usually contains the word "request" in its e-mail address (example: hang-gliding-request@lists.utah.edu).

Join a List

When you want to join a manually maintained list, make sure you find out what information the administrator needs and include the information in your message.

Automated Lists

A computer program manages an automated mailing list. There are three popular programs that manage automated lists—listproc, listserv and majordomo.

An automated list typically contains the name of the program that manages the list in its e-mail address (example: majordomo@teleport.com).

Join a List

When you want to join an automated list, make sure you find out what information the program needs and include the information in your message. If a program does not understand your message, it may not respond to your request.

MAILING LIST RESTRICTIONS

Restricted Mailing Lists

Some mailing lists restrict the number of people allowed to join. If you want to join one of these lists, you may have to wait for someone else to leave the list.

Other mailing lists require that you meet certain qualifications to join. For example, a mailing list about surgery may be restricted to medical doctors.

Moderated Mailing Lists

Some mailing lists are moderated. A volunteer reads each message sent to a moderated list and decides if the message is appropriate for the list. If the message is appropriate, the volunteer sends the message to every person on the mailing list.

A moderated mailing list keeps discussions on topic and removes messages containing ideas already discussed.

In an unmoderated mailing list, all messages are automatically sent to everyone on the list.

Mailing list etiquette refers to the proper way to behave when sending messages to a mailing list.

Mailing List Etiquette

READ MESSAGES

Read the messages in a mailing list for a week before sending a message. This is a good way to learn how people in a mailing list communicate and prevents you from submitting inappropriate information or information already discussed.

WRITING STYLE

Hundreds of people may read a message you send to a mailing list. Before sending a message, make sure you carefully reread the message.

Make sure your message is clear, concise and contains no spelling or grammar errors.

Also make sure your message will not be misinterpreted. For example, not all readers will realize a statement is meant to be sarcastic.

SUBJECT

The subject of a message is the first item people read. Make sure the subject clearly identifies the contents of the message. For example, the subject "Read this now" or "For your information" is not very informative.

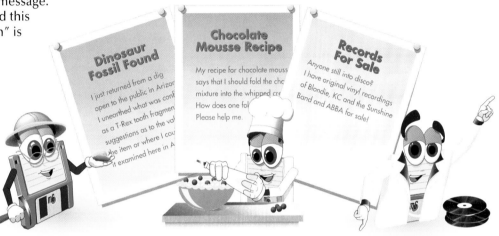

REPLY TO MESSAGES

You can reply to a message to answer a question, express an opinion or supply additional information. Reply to a message only when you have something important to say. A reply such as "Me too" or "I agree" is not very useful.

Quoting

When you reply to a message, make sure you include some of the original message. This is called quoting. Quoting helps readers identify which message you are replying to. To save readers time, make sure you delete all parts of the original message that do not directly relate to your reply.

Private Replies

If your reply would not be of interest to others in a mailing list or if you want to send a private response, send a message to the author instead of sending your reply to the entire mailing list.

2000ad-l

Discussion of the millennial year 2000.
Contact: listproc@usc.edu

Type in message:
subscribe 2000ad-l *Your Name*

Dinosaur

Discussion of dinosaurs and other prehistoric animals.
Contact: listproc@usc.edu

Type in message:
subscribe dinosaur *Your Name*

A.Word.A.Day

Sends you a word and its definition every day.
Contact: wsmith@wordsmith.org

Type in subject line:
subscribe *Your Name*

Ghost Stories

Ghost stories and other spooky discussions.
Contact: ghost-stories-request@
    aurora.cdb.com

Choco

Sends you a collection of chocolate recipes once a month.
Contact: majordomo@apk.net

Type in message:
subscribe choco

Kidsbooks

Reviews of children's books.
Contact: kidsbooks-request@
    armory.com

Diabetic

Where diabetics can exchange ideas and comments.
Contact: listserv@lehigh.edu

Type in message:
subscribe diabetic *Your Name*

Melrose Place

Discussion of the popular television series.
Contact: majordomo@tcp.com

Type in message:
subscribe melrose-place

Movie Review

A resource for movie reviews.
Contact: moviereview–request@
    cuenet.com

Type in message:
subscribe

Tennis Server Interactive

Monthly tennis news, tips
and notices.
Contact: racquet-notices-request
    @tennisserver.com

NA–Soccer

Discussion of North American soccer.
Contact: majordomo@hoplite.org

Type in message:
subscribe na–soccer

Veggie

Discussion of issues relevant
to vegetarians.
Contact: veggie-request@
    maths.bath.ac.uk

Offroad

Information and discussions
about 4x4 and offroad driving.
Contact: offroad-request@
    off-road.com

Vintage Music

Discussion of older music, such
as early jazz and blues, big bands,
show music, vaudeville and
classical music.
Contact: listproc@cornell.edu

Pen Pals

A place for children to correspond
on the Internet.
Contact: pen-pals-request
    @mainstream.com

Weights

Discussion of all aspects
of weightlifting.
Contact: weights-request@
    fa.disney.com

CHAPTER 5

NEWSGROUPS

What are newsgroups and what are the main categories of newsgroups? In this chapter you will learn how newsgroups allow people around the world with common interests to communicate with each other.

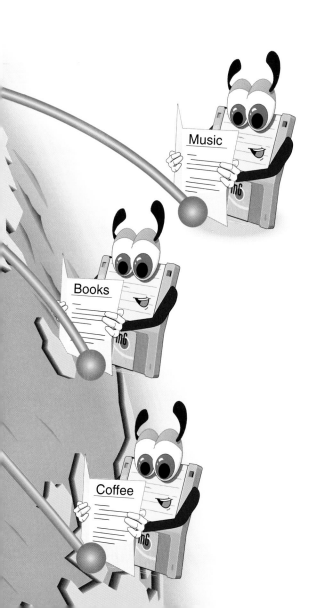

INTRODUCTION TO NEWSGROUPS

biz.jobs.offered   **rec.puzzles**   **sci.med.pharmacy**

A newsgroup is a discussion group that allows people with common interests to communicate with each other.

There are thousands of newsgroups on every subject imaginable. Each newsgroup discusses a particular topic such as jobs offered, puzzles or medicine.

Usenet, short for Users' Network, refers to all the computers that are connected to distribute newsgroup information.

NEWSGROUP NAMES

The name of a newsgroup describes the type of information discussed in the newsgroup. A newsgroup name consists of two or more words, separated by periods (.).

The first word describes the main topic (example: **rec** for recreation). Each of the following words narrows the topic.

ARTICLES

A newsgroup can contain hundreds or thousands of articles.

Article

An article is a message an individual posts, or sends, to a newsgroup. An article can be a few lines of text or the length of a book.

Thread

A thread is an article and all replies to the article. A thread may include an initial question and the responses from other readers.

SORTING ARTICLES

When displaying a list of articles in a newsgroup, you can usually view several pieces of information about the articles. This information includes the name of the person who wrote the article, the subject of the article and the date the article was sent to the newsgroup.

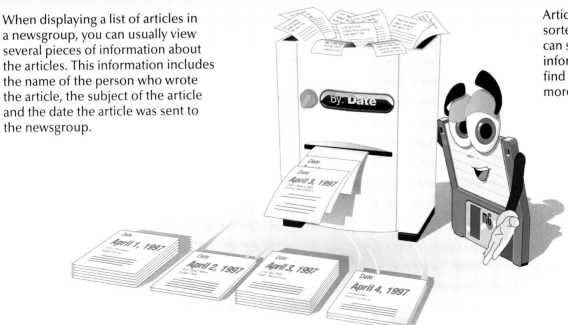

Articles are most often sorted by date, but you can sort articles by other information to help you find articles of interest more easily.

Web Browsers

Many Web browsers have a newsreader built-in. This means the look and feel of the newsreader is very similar to the look and feel of the Web browser. If you are familiar with using the Web browser, you should find the built-in newsreader easy to learn and use. Newsreaders built into Web browsers often do not have as many features as separate newsreader programs.

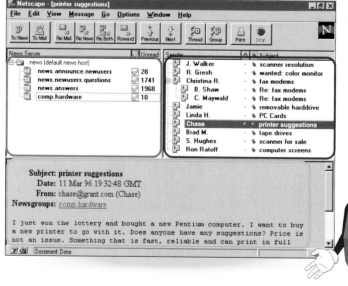

■ This area displays a list of newsgroups.

■ This area displays a list of all the articles in the selected newsgroup.

▥ This area displays the contents of a single article.

Kill Files

Most newsreaders allow you to enter the name of a person into a file called a kill file. This tells the newsreader to automatically delete any articles posted by that person. Kill files are useful when someone is frequently posting inappropriate articles to a newsgroup.

Filters

Some newsgroups can receive over a thousand articles in one day. Some newsreaders provide filters that allow you to display only the type of articles you want to read.

This lets you find the information you need without having to read every article in the newsgroup.

Privacy

There are many companies that index all articles posted to Usenet newsgroups. This allows people on the Internet to search the indexed articles and monitor which newsgroups you post to and how often you post articles.

To keep your articles private, some newsreaders now let you automatically mark an article so it will not be indexed by search companies.

You subscribe to a newsgroup you want to read on a regular basis.

If you no longer want to read the articles in a newsgroup, you can unsubscribe from the newsgroup at any time.

Moderated Newsgroups

Some newsgroups are moderated. In these newsgroups, a volunteer reads each article and decides if the article is appropriate for the newsgroup. If the article is appropriate, the volunteer posts the article for everyone to read.

Moderated newsgroups may have the word "moderated" at the end of the newsgroup name (example: **sci.military.moderated**).

In an unmoderated newsgroup, all articles are automatically posted for everyone to read.

New Newsgroups

New newsgroups are created every day. A newsreader lets you display a list of all the newsgroups that have been created since the last time you checked.

Once you have the names of new newsgroups, you can subscribe to the newsgroups.

Similar Newsgroups

There is often more than one newsgroup that discusses a particular topic. For example, the topics discussed in the **alt.books.reviews** newsgroup are similar to the topics discussed in **rec.arts.books**.

If you are interested in a specific topic, you should subscribe to all the newsgroups that discuss the topic.

Removed Newsgroups

When a newsgroup becomes very popular, it is often removed and split into several smaller, more specific groups. For example, a newsgroup for buying and selling items might be split into two smaller newsgroups: one for computer-related items and the other for non-computer-related items.

If a newsgroup you are subscribed to is removed, you may be able to subscribe to the new, smaller newsgroups.

WORK WITH ARTICLES

READ AN ARTICLE

You can read articles to learn the opinions and ideas of thousands of people around the world.

New articles are sent to newsgroups every day. You can browse through articles of interest just as you would browse through the morning newspaper.

PRINT AN ARTICLE

You can produce a paper copy of an article you find interesting.

POST AN ARTICLE

You can post, or send, a new article to a newsgroup to ask a question or express an opinion. Thousands of people around the world may read an article you post.

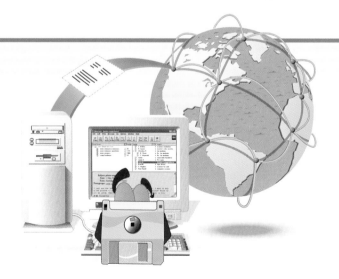

If you want to practice posting an article, send an article to the **alt.test** newsgroup. You will receive automated replies to let you know you posted correctly. Do not send practice articles to other newsgroups.

REPLY TO AN ARTICLE

You can reply to an article to answer a question, express an opinion or supply additional information. A reply you post to a newsgroup is called a follow-up.

Reply to an article only when you have something important to say. A reply such as "Me too" or "I agree" is not very informative.

Original Article

I am a vampire and I want to meet others like me. Call me at (613) 555-2632. But don't call after 10 because it will wake up my parents.

Reply

I am a vampire and I want to meet others like me. Call me at (613) 555-2632. But don't call after 10 because it will wake up my parents.
I am a vampire too. Let's meet for a bite and a drink. Call (613) 555-7575.

Quoting

When you reply to an article, make sure you include part of the original article. This is called quoting. Quoting helps readers identify which article you are replying to. To save readers time, make sure you delete all parts of the original article that do not directly relate to your reply.

Private Replies

If your reply would not be of interest to others in a newsgroup or if you want to send a private response, send a message to the author instead of posting your reply to the entire newsgroup.

Verify E-Mail Address

Some companies collect e-mail addresses from articles posted to newsgroups and use these addresses to distribute advertisements. To avoid receiving this junk mail, you can make small changes, such as typing "at" instead of the @ symbol, when specifying your e-mail address in an article. When companies try to send you advertisements, the messages will not be delivered. Always correct these intentional mistakes in an author's e-mail address when you reply to the author of an article, otherwise your response will not be delivered.

ENCODE ARTICLES

UUENCODE

An article can contain information other than text, such as a graphic or sound recording. To send this type of information to a newsgroup, you need to use uuencode software. Uuencode software lets you convert a graphic or sound recording so it can travel across the Internet. Most newsreaders have built-in uuencode software.

ROT13

ROT13 lets you turn a newsgroup article you post into a string of meaningless characters. This prevents others from reading information that may be offensive or a spoiler, such as the ending of a movie.

ROT13 works by transposing each letter in an article by 13 characters. For example, the letter "a" becomes the letter "n."

Gur raqvat bs gur zbivr vf vaperqvoyr! Wnpbo naq Anapl svanyyl ernpu gur gbc bs Zbhag Rirerfg, naq ur cebcbfrf gb ure. Anapl npprcgf!

The ending of the movie is incredible! Jacob and Nancy finally reach the top of Mount Everest, and he proposes to her. Nancy accepts!

If you want to read an article encoded using ROT13, you must first decode the text. Some news readers can decode articles for you.

A news server is a computer that stores newsgroup articles.

News servers are maintained by service providers, which are companies that give you access to the Internet.

The newsgroups available to you depend on your service provider. Your service provider may limit the available newsgroups to save valuable storage space.

When you send an article to a newsgroup, the news server you are connected to keeps a copy of the article and then distributes the article to other news servers around the world.

The amount of information sent to newsgroups each day is approximately equal to the amount of information in a set of encyclopedias.

After a few days or weeks, articles are removed from a news server to make room for new articles. When you see an article you want to keep, make sure you print or save the article.

NEWSGROUP ETIQUETTE

Writing Style

Thousands of people around the world may read an article you post to a newsgroup. Before posting an article, make sure you carefully reread the article.

ARTICLE

I just won the lottery. I bought a new Pentium computer. I want to buy a new printer to go with it. Does anyone has any suggestions? Price is probably not an issue but it might be. I would prefer something that are fast, reliable and can print in full color. Thanks in advance.

⟳ -Grammar errors
? -Misleading

Make sure your article is clear, concise and contains no spelling or grammar errors.

Also make sure your article will not be misinterpreted. For example, not all readers will realize a statement is meant to be sarcastic.

Subject

The subject of an article is the first item people read. Make sure your subject clearly identifies the contents of your article.

For example, the subject "Read this now" or "For your information" is not very informative.

Baseball Teams

I live in the Seattle area and was wondering if anyone knows where I can join an adult baseball team.

Thanks!
mG

Read Articles

Read the articles in a newsgroup for a week before posting an article. This is called lurking. Lurking is a good way to learn how people in a newsgroup communicate and prevents you from posting information others have already read.

Read the FAQ

The FAQ (Frequently Asked Questions) is a document containing a list of questions and answers that often appear in a newsgroup.

The FAQ is designed to prevent new readers from asking questions that have already been answered. Make sure you read the FAQ before posting any articles to a newsgroup.

Post to the Appropriate Newsgroup

Make sure you post an article to the appropriate newsgroup. This ensures that people interested in your questions and comments will see your article.

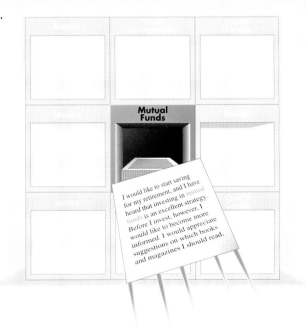

Do not post an article to several inappropriate newsgroups. This is called spamming. Spamming is particularly annoying when the article serves a commercial purpose, such as selling a product or service.

MAIN NEWSGROUP CATEGORIES

Newsgroups are divided into separate sections, or categories. The newsgroups in each category discuss the same general topic. Newsgroup categories are also referred to as the Newsgroup Hierarchy.

alt (alternative)

General interest discussions that can include unusual or bizarre topics. Some of the material available in the **alt** newsgroups may be offensive to some people.

biz (business)

Business discussions that are usually more commercial in nature than those in other newsgroups. Advertising is allowed in many **biz** newsgroups and lists of job openings are available.

comp (computers)

Discussions of computer hardware, software and computer science. The **comp** newsgroups are a good source of technical support for computer-related problems.

misc (miscellaneous)

Discussions of various topics that may overlap topics discussed in other categories. Many of the topics discussed in the **misc** newsgroups can also be found in the alt newsgroups.

rec (recreation)

Discussions of recreational activities and hobbies. The messages in the **rec** newsgroups are often more entertaining than informative.

soc (social)

Discussions of social issues, including world cultures and political topics. The **soc** newsgroups also contain information about selected regions around the world.

CHAPTER 6

CHAT

Why is chatting one of the most popular features of the Internet? This chapter introduces you to Web-based chat, voice chat, video chat and much more.

INTRODUCTION TO CHAT

You can instantly communicate with people around the world by typing back and forth. This is called chatting. Chatting is one of the most frequently used features of the Internet.

TYPES OF CHAT

Text-Based

Text-based chat is the oldest and most popular type of chat on the Internet. You can have conversations with one or more people. When you type text, the text appears on the screen of each person participating in the conversation.

Since text transfers quickly across the Internet, you do not need a high-speed connection to the Internet.

```
Tanya - I need some help! I have to write
an essay about an unusual animal. Any
ideas?

Chris - How about the dodo bird?

Robin - My teacher assigned me the same
project and I couldn't find any info on
the dodo bird.

Chris - What animal did you write about?

Robin - I wrote about the sea cucumber.
It's unusual and there is lots of info out
there.
```

Multimedia

Multimedia chat is one of the newer features of the Internet. You can now have voice conversations and communicate with other people through live video over the Internet. Since sound and video transfer slowly across the Internet, you should have a high-speed connection to use multimedia chat.

Education

Many students use chat to discuss assignments and get help from fellow students and instructors. This is particularly useful for people who are too far away from schools or colleges to attend classes on a regular basis.

Entertainment

Most people use chat as a form of entertainment. You can use chat to meet new friends from all over the world.

Keep in Touch

Chatting is a low-cost way to stay in touch with friends or relatives who have access to the Internet. Many people use Internet chat to communicate with friends and family members in other parts of the world.

Product Support

Some product manufacturers are now using Internet chat to provide technical support for their customers. Technical support people make themselves available for chatting so customers can ask questions and get answers instantly.

INTERNET RELAY CHAT

Internet Relay Chat (IRC) is a system that allows you to chat with other people on the Internet. To use IRC, you must connect to a computer called an IRC server. Each IRC server is connected to a network of other IRC servers around the world.

IRC Chat

<Greg> I would like to fill my apartment with plants but I have such a hard time growing them. I certainly wasn't born with a green thumb.

<Brenda> Well, why don't you buy a cactus? They are easy to grow.

<John> I agree. A cactus is simple to care for. It only needs water once a month.

<Michael> And a cactus will grow well with little light.

<Greg> If I decide to buy a cactus, what kind should I choose?

<Michael> Well, I like the Desert Gold variety.

<John> Yes, they're attractive. But handle with care; their spines are quite sharp.

<Greg> Great, the only plant I can grow is the kind that bites!

Name and E-Mail Address

Before connecting to IRC, you must enter your name and e-mail address. Most IRC servers will not let you connect unless you enter a valid e-mail address. You can enter a fake name if you wish to remain anonymous, but other people may still be able to find out your real name.

Nicknames

You must choose a nickname for yourself before using IRC. If another person is already using your nickname, you must choose a different nickname. A nickname can have up to nine letters. You can often register your nickname so no one else can use the nickname.

Channels

There are many channels, or chat groups, you can join on IRC. Each channel usually focuses on a specific topic. A channel name often tells you the theme of the discussion.

A # symbol in front of a channel name means the channel is available to people all over the world.

An & symbol in front of a channel name means the channel is available only to people using the IRC server you are connected to.

Channel Operators

If you try to join a channel that does not exist, IRC will create a new channel and make you the channel operator. When you leave the channel, you are no longer the channel operator.

A channel operator controls who may join the channel. Channel operator nicknames display the @ symbol. Some channels are permanently controlled by programs called "bots," which is short for robots.

CONNECT TO IRC

An IRC network is a group of IRC servers located all over the world that are connected together to allow people to chat. There are many IRC networks you can connect to.

EFNet

EFNet is the largest of all the IRC networks and has the most unruly users.

http://www.efnet.org

Undernet

Undernet is a smaller version of EFNet. Undernet users tend to be more friendly than EFNet users.

http://www.undernet.org

DALnet

DALnet is an IRC network where you can permanently register your own nickname and leave messages for other people.

http://www.dal.net

NewNet

Unlike other IRC networks, NewNet allows users to vote on issues that involve changes to the network.

http://www.newnet.net

Different IRC networks are not connected to each other. This means that if you want to chat with people on an EFNet IRC channel, you must connect to the EFNet network.

IRC PROGRAMS

You need an IRC program to be able to connect to a server on an IRC network.

Most IRC programs are very easy to use and provide many features you can customize to suit your needs. For example, some IRC programs allow you to change the font and color of the text that appears on your screen to make the text easier to read.

There are many IRC programs available on the World Wide Web. You can try these programs free of charge for a limited time:

Ircle (Macintosh)
http://www.xs4all.nl/~ircle

mIRC (Windows)
http://www.mirc.co.uk

PIRCH (Windows)
http://www.bcpl.lib.md.us/
~frappa/pirch.html

Just like at a cocktail party, there is a proper way to behave when chatting with people on IRC. Ignoring IRC etiquette could get you disconnected or permanently banned from the IRC server.

Respect Language

People from many different countries use IRC. This means many channels might be used by people who do not speak the same language as you. When you join a channel, respect the language being used in the channel. If you want to discuss the topic in your own language, start a new channel for people who speak the same language as you.

Automatic Greetings

Many software programs allow you to automatically say hello to anyone new who joins the channel you are in. These automatic greetings are not appreciated by users of IRC. Only greet people if you know them or wish to start chatting with them.

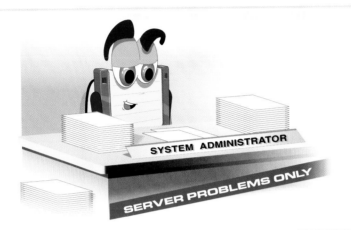

Complaining to IRC Administrators

Each IRC channel has a channel operator who can ban people from the channel for any reason. If you have been banned from a channel, do not complain to the system administrator of the IRC server. These IRC administrators are responsible for maintaining the servers and do not have time to settle disputes between IRC users.

Flooding

Sending a lot of text to a channel at once is called flooding. Many IRC programs have built-in controls to restrict the amount of information you can send at once.

If you flood a channel, you may be disconnected or permanently banned from the IRC server.

Cloning

You can easily start several IRC programs on your computer and connect to IRC using different nicknames. This is known as "cloning." Since cloning is often used to cause mischief, many IRC servers can now find out if you are connected using a different nickname.

Cloning may cause you to be banned from using the IRC server in the future.

Smiley   Bill   Ann   Chuckles   Bob   Blondie

> Web-based chat is one of the newer features of the Internet. Web-based chat is fun and easy to use.

Web Browser

All the chat networks on the World Wide Web require only that you have a Web browser to participate. Some chat Web sites use newer features such as Java.

If you have trouble participating in a Web-based chat site, make sure you have the latest version of your Web browser.

Cost

Most of the chat services on the Web are free. Many of the Web-based chat sites receive income from companies that advertise on the Web sites.

This means the chat sites do not have to charge users. Some chat services allow you to participate for free for a limited time, but then you must pay a fee to continue chatting.

CHAT WEB SITES

WebChat Broadcasting System

WebChat claims to be the largest Web-based chat network on the Internet. WebChat often offers chat rooms hosted by experts such as personal finance counselors and travel consultants.

You can access WebChat at the following Web site:

http://www.wbs.net

Ichat

Ichat is very similar to Internet Relay Chat. When you enter text, anyone in the same chat room, or group, will see the text you entered. Ichat is much easier to set up and use than Internet Relay Chat.

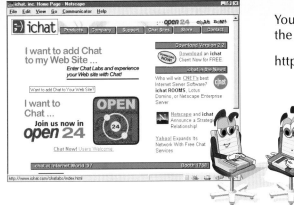

You can access Ichat at the following Web site:

http://www.ichat.com

3-D CHAT

Worlds Chat

Worlds Chat allows you to walk around and talk to other people in a three-dimensional world. People are represented by objects, such as penguins and chess pieces, known as avatars.

You must have the Worlds Chat software before you can chat in Worlds Chat. You can get the Worlds Chat software at the following Web site:

http://www.worlds.net

VOICE CHAT

Voice chat over the Internet lets you hear the voices of friends, family and colleagues around the world without paying any long-distance telephone charges.

You need an Internet phone program to talk over the Internet. You can get a trial version of Internet phone software at the following Web sites:

Intel
http://www.intel.com/iaweb/cpc/iphone

VocalTec
http://www.vocaltec.com

Equipment

You need specific equipment to talk over the Internet. Your computer must have a sound card with speakers and a microphone attached. A half-duplex sound card lets only one person talk at a time. A full-duplex sound card lets two people talk at once, just as you would talk on the telephone. Full-duplex sound cards are the best type of sound card for voice chat.

Contact Other People

If you want to communicate with another person using voice chat, you must both use the same type of Internet phone software. You can usually find a directory of people who use your Internet phone program at the Web site where you got the program. You can browse through the directory to find people you want to chat with.

Video chat lets you see the person you are talking to, even if the other person is on the other side of the world. You can also talk to several people at once.

You need a special program to communicate using video chat on the Internet. You can get a trial version of video chat software at the following Web sites:

CU-SeeMe
http://goliath.wpine.com/cu-seeme.html

V-Fone
http://www.summersoft.com

To communicate with other people using video chat, everyone must use the same type of video chat software.

Equipment

Before you can use video chat, you must have a video camera for your computer. You can buy an inexpensive video camera that attaches to the top of your monitor. You can also use a regular video camera if you have a special expansion card for your computer.

Image Quality

If you are using a modem to transfer video images, the quality of the images may be poor. Some video chat programs can help increase the quality of video images. Make sure you try out a video chat program before purchasing to see the quality of the images.

#beginner
Help for Internet beginners.

#chatzone
General discussions and chitchat.

#café
A relaxing place to hang out.

#geek
Where computer addicts can be found.

#cars
Discussions about all types of cars.

#history
General and specific discussions about history.

#cats
All things to do with cats.

#international
Where people from different nations gather.

#ircnewbies
Ask questions
about IRC chat.

#nhl
National Hockey
League.

#mlb
Major League
Baseball.

#pcgames
Talk about games for
home computers.

#nba
National
Basketball
Association.

#politics
Chat about politics
around the world.

#new2irc
This should be
your first stop
on IRC.

#windows
Discussions about the
Microsoft Windows
operating systems.

CHAPTER 7

FTP

What is FTP and why is it useful? In this chapter you will learn how FTP allows you to search for information on computers around the world.

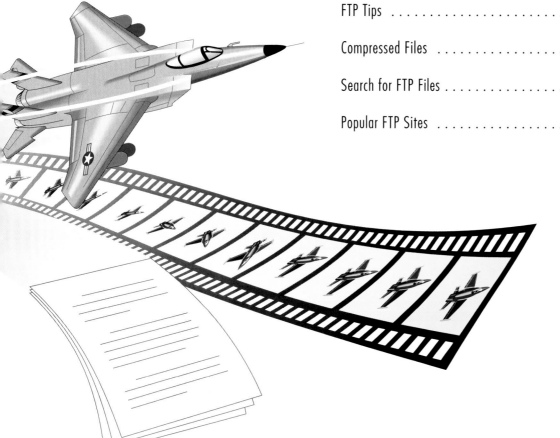

INTRODUCTION TO FTP

File Transfer Protocol (FTP) lets you look through files stored on computers around the world and copy files that interest you.

FTP SITE

An FTP site is a computer on the Internet that stores files. FTP sites are maintained by colleges, universities, government agencies, companies and individuals. There are thousands of FTP sites scattered across the Internet.

Private FTP Sites

Some FTP sites are private and require you to enter a password before you can access any files. Many corporations maintain private FTP sites to make files available to their employees and clients around the world.

Anonymous FTP Sites

Many FTP sites are anonymous. Anonymous FTP sites let you access files without entering a password. These sites store huge collections of files that anyone can download, or copy, free of charge.

Files at FTP sites are stored in different directories.

Directories

Just as folders organize documents in a filing cabinet, directories organize information at an FTP site.

Most FTP sites have a main directory called **pub**, which is short for public. The pub directory contains subdirectories and files.

Most subdirectory names indicate what type of files the subdirectory contains. Common subdirectory names include **apps** for application programs and **docs** for text files and documents.

File Names

Every file stored at an FTP site has a name and an extension, separated by a period (.). The name describes the contents of a file. The extension usually identifies the type of file.

Most well-established FTP sites include files that describe the rest of the files offered at the site. Look for files named "readme" or "index".

TYPES OF FILES

Text

You can get interesting documents for research and for enjoyment. You can obtain books, journals, electronic magazines, computer manuals, government documents, news summaries and academic papers.

Look for these extensions:

.asc .doc .htm .html
.msg .txt .wpd

Images

You can get images, such as computer-generated art, museum paintings and pictures of famous people.

Look for these extensions:

.bmp .eps .gif .jpg .pict .png

Sound

You can get theme songs, sound effects, clips of famous speeches and lines from television shows and movies.

Look for these extensions:

.au .ra .ram .snd .wav

Video

You can get movie clips, cartoons, educational videos and computer-generated animation.

Look for these extensions:

.avi .mov .mpg

Programs

You can get programs to use on your computer, such as word processors, spreadsheets, databases, games and much more.

Look for these extensions:

.bat .com .exe

Public Domain

Public domain programs are free and have no copyright restrictions. You can change and distribute public domain programs as you wish.

Freeware

Freeware programs are free but have copyright restrictions. The author may require you to follow certain rules if you want to change or distribute freeware programs.

Shareware

You can try a shareware program free of charge for a limited time. If you like the program and want to continue using it, you must pay the author of the program.

Avoid Traffic Jams

Each FTP site can only let a certain number of people use the site at once. If you get an error message when you try to connect, the site may already have as many people connected as it can handle.

Connect at a Different Time

Try accessing FTP sites outside business hours, such as at night and on the weekend. Fewer people use the Internet at these times.

Use Mirror Sites

Some popular FTP sites have mirror sites. A mirror site stores exactly the same information as the original site but is usually less busy. A mirror site may also be geographically closer to your computer, which can provide a faster and more reliable connection.

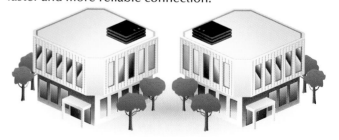

Mirror sites are updated on a regular basis to ensure that the files available at the original site are also available at the mirror site.

Compatibility

Just because you can transfer a file to your computer does not mean you can use the file. Make sure you only get files that can work with your type of computer. Many FTP sites have separate directories for Macintosh and IBM-compatible computers.

Hardware and Software

You may need special hardware or software to use files you get from an FTP site. For example, you need a sound card and speakers to hear sound files.

Viruses

Files stored at FTP sites may contain viruses. A virus is a destructive computer program that can disrupt the normal operation of a computer.

You should frequently make backup copies of the files on your computer and always check for viruses before you use any file copied from an FTP site.

Anti-virus programs are available at most major FTP sites.

> Many large files stored at FTP sites are compressed, or squeezed, to make them smaller.

Compressed Files

A smaller, compressed file requires less storage space and travels more quickly across the Internet.

Compressed or archived files usually have one of the following extensions:

.arc   .arj   .gz   .hqx   .sit   .tar   .z   .zip

Archived Files

A program usually consists of a large group of files. Programs are often compressed and then packaged (archived) into a single file. This prevents you from having to transfer each file individually to your computer.

Decompressed Files

Before you can use a compressed or archived file on your computer, you usually have to expand or unpack the file using a decompression program.

You can often get a decompression program for free at sites where you copy files. Popular decompression programs include PKZip for IBM-compatible computers and StuffIt for Macintosh computers.

SEARCH FOR FTP FILES

There are sites that let you search for files available at FTP sites around the world. This helps you find files of interest to you.

ARCHIE

Archie lets you search for specific files you have heard or read about. To use Archie, you need to know part of the name of the file you want to find.

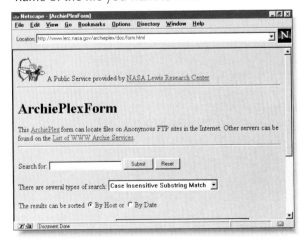

Archie is available at the following Web sites:

NASA
http://www.lerc.nasa.gov/archieplex

Rutgers University
http://www-ns.rutgers.edu/htbin/archie

SHAREWARE.COM

Shareware.com lets you search for specific files or browse through files stored at FTP sites around the world.

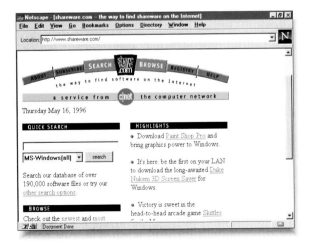

You can access shareware.com at the following Web site:

http://www.shareware.com

Anonymous FTP Server

At this site you can find listings of other FTP sites available on the Internet.

iraun1.ira.uka.de

Mcafee Software

This FTP site contains shareware programs that protect your computer against viruses.

ftp.mcafee.com

Conjelco

This FTP site contains many files for fans of casino gaming and card games.

ftp.conjelco.com

mirror.apple.com

You can find an extensive collection of software and information for Macintosh computers at this site.

mirror.apple.com#beginner

Help for Internet beginners.

The INESC Archive

This site hosts electronic text versions of the complete works of William Shakespeare.

porthos.inescn.pt/pub/doc/ Fiction/Shakespeare

OAK Software Repository

One of the most popular FTP sites on the Internet, this site contains all types of programs for many types of computers.

oak.oakland.edu

LEO - Link Everything Online

This site stores all types of information about music and related topics, including a collection of song lyrics.

ftp.leo.org/pub

ServiceTech

You can find a collection of all sorts of software programs and text files at this FTP site.

ftp.servtech.com

TSX-11

This Massachusetts Institute of Technology FTP site contains a wide range of information and software.

tsx-11.mit.edu

Walnut Creek CD-ROM

This site provides a collection of software and information that is also available at computer stores on CD-ROM discs.

ftp.cdrom.com

University of Nevada

This site contains a lot of useful information for photographers.

ftp.nevada.edu/pub/photo

Windows FTP Archive

A collection of shareware and freeware programs for computers that use a Windows operating system.

ftp.winsite.com

Usenet FAQ Directory

This FTP site provides a collection of all the available FAQs for Usenet newsgroups.

rtfm.mit.edu/pub/usenet-by-group

The World

One of the oldest sites available on the Internet, The World site contains a wide variety of documents.

ftp.std.com

Vaasa University, Finland

A huge collection of programs and information files for all types of computers can be found at this site.

garbo.uwasa.fi

Ziff-Davis

This FTP site contains files from popular computing magazines such as PC Week and PC Magazine.

ftp.zdnet.com

CHAPTER 8

MULTI-PLAYER GAMES

What types of multi-player games are available? In this chapter you will learn about traditional multi-player games, multi-user dungeons, commercial software games and much more.

A multi-player game is a game that lets you use a computer to play against one or more opponents. Multi-player games are becoming one of the most popular uses of the Internet.

Types

There are many types of multi-player games on the Internet. One of the simplest types is Play By E-Mail (PBEM) games, where players simply e-mail their moves to other players. Arcade-style games are also very popular. You can play fast-paced action or adventure games against players on the other side of the world.

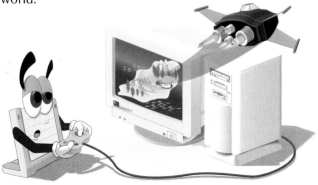

Flexible

There are hundreds of multi-player games you can play over the Internet. Everyone can find a game that suits their interests. You can find games that require several hours a day or just a few minutes each week. You can choose from simple card games to complex games requiring science and math skills.

Interactive

Playing multi-player games on the Internet allows you to interact and communicate with people from all over the world. Some games even have their own associations where players can meet each other face to face.

Challenging

Even though you can play most games against a computer, many games are better when you play them against other people. Most computers react the same way each time you play a game. When you play a game against a person, the game will be different every time.

Competitive

Playing games on the Internet can be very competitive. Almost every game played on the Internet has a site on the World Wide Web that displays a list of winners.

Some games even have tournaments for the top players of the game.

PLAY BY E-MAIL GAMES

Play By E-Mail (PBEM) games are a convenient and simple way to participate in multi-player games. To play an e-mail game, you need an e-mail account set up on your computer.

Move 10:
White bishop B6 to F2

Types of Games

There are several types of e-mail games. To play the simplest type, such as chess or checkers, you exchange moves with your opponent by e-mail. In more complex types of games, all the players e-mail their moves to one computer. The computer processes all the moves and controls the flow of the game.

Benefits

E-mail games allow each player to play at a convenient time, so you do not have to constantly be at your computer to play. You can also easily find an opponent whose skill level matches your skill level. Playing people with similar skill levels usually makes games more fun.

POPULAR E-MAIL GAMES

Global Diplomacy

Global Diplomacy is a strategy game where you attempt to conquer the world. Each player controls a region of the world. You must negotiate and make pacts with other players to win the game.

You can find out more about Global Diplomacy at the following Web site:

http://www.islandnet.com/ ~dgreenin/emg-game.htm#GD

Food Chain

This mathematics-based game allows you to design your own species of animal or plant and then release it into the jungle. Depending on how well you designed the species, it will either evolve or become extinct.

You can find out more about Food Chain at the following Web site:

http://www.pbm.com/~lindahl/ pbm_list/descriptions/ food_chain.html

Electronic Knock Out

In this game, you are the manager of a group of boxers. You control the characteristics of each boxer in your group. Each week you submit your boxers for fights against boxers controlled by other players.

You can find out more about Electronic Knock Out at the following Web site:

http://www.vivi.com

TRADITIONAL MULTI-PLAYER GAMES

Some of the first games to be played on the Internet were traditional board and card games, such as backgammon and bridge.

Players

Most traditional multi-player games are board or card games. When you play these types of games on the Internet, you can quickly find opponents and start a game. You can play these games with friends and family members, even if they are located on the other side of the world.

How about a game of cards?

Board Games

Many people find it difficult to play board games when the board is displayed on a computer monitor. To avoid this problem, you can set up the game board in front of your computer. You can then move the game pieces on the board according to what appears on your computer screen.

TRADITIONAL GAMES

Backgammon

There are many places on the Internet where you can play backgammon. The WWW Backgammon Page has information about backgammon and provides links to help you play with other people on the Internet.

The WWW Backgammon Page is located at:

http://www.gamesdomain.com/backgammon

Bridge

Bridge is one of the most popular card games in the world. You can use the Internet to learn and practice the game. When you are ready to play against a real person, you can easily find an opponent on the Internet.

You can find more information about bridge on the Internet at:

http://www.bridgeplayer.com

Chess

Chess is one of the oldest games in the world. When you play chess on the Internet, you can easily find an opponent whose skill level matches your skill level.

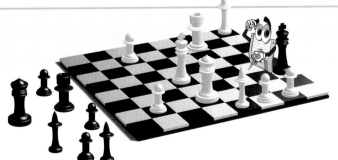

The Internet Chess Club hosts over 15,000 chess matches each day. The Internet Chess Club is located at:

http://www.hydra.com/icc

Multi-User Dungeons (MUDs) are one of the oldest and most popular forms of multi-player games on the Internet. MUDs allow you to interact with other people in a variety of different worlds.

Virtual Worlds

MUDs take place in virtual worlds. When you play a MUD, you assume the identity of a character living in the virtual world. You type commands to make your character perform actions like running or talking. You also type commands to make changes to the world, such as creating or destroying buildings.

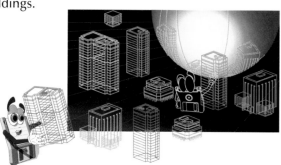

MUSHs, MOOs and MUCKs

MUSHs, MOOs and MUCKs are types of MUDs. The name of each type refers to the type of software that runs the MUD. MUSHs, MOOs and MUCKs each use their own commands to perform tasks in the virtual world. Each type of MUD also has its own set of rules. Some types let you fight with other characters, while other types do not.

POPULAR MUDS

London by Gaslight

This game is set in London, England at the turn of the century, during the time of Jack the Ripper, Sherlock Holmes and Dr. Jekyll and Mr. Hyde.

Find out more about London by Gaslight at:

http://www.ultranet.com/~rogerc/lbg_intro.html

Masquerade

This game is for fans of vampires, werewolves and things that go bump in the night.

Find out more about Masquerade at:

http://www.iquest.net/bc/masq

VenusMUSH

This game is set in the year 2041, when all the inhabitants of Earth have relocated to the planet Venus and are governed by an alien race.

Find out more about VenusMUSH at:

http://mama.indstate.edu/users/bones/venus/Venus.html

AuroraMUSH

AuroraMUSH is a pleasant place to visit with a very social theme. Players are encouraged to interact with other characters.

Find out more about AuroraMUSH at:

http://galaxy.neca.com/~soruk

COMMERCIAL SOFTWARE GAMES

Often when you buy a commercial software game, you can only play the game against the computer. Many games now let you play against other people on the Internet.

Get Software

You can buy commercial software games at many computer stores. There are also many commercial software games available on the Internet. If you are playing a commercial software game with other people, each person must have their own copy of the game.

Connecting

Connecting to other people on the Internet to play a commercial software game is often very simple. Commercial software games are usually played on one computer on the Internet. To play the game, you simply connect to this computer.

POPULAR COMMERCIAL GAMES

Quake

Quake is one of the most popular commercial software games. In this three-dimensional game, you walk around computer-generated worlds looking for your enemies. Up to 16 people can participate in a game.

You can find more information about Quake at the following location:

http://www.idsoftware.com

Command & Conquer

Command & Conquer is a military strategy game you can play with up to three other people at a time.

You can find more information about Command & Conquer at the following Web site:

http://www.westwood.com

Big Red Racing

Big Red Racing lets you race against up to five different people at a time. You can choose strange vehicles to race in, such as a snow plow or a boat.

You can find more information about Big Red Racing at:

http://www.worldserver.pipex. com/bigred/racing/index.html

CHAPTER 9

INTERESTING WEB SITES

Would you like to visit some great Web sites? This chapter includes a variety of unique Web sites you can visit.

lp

ı Vert

re ressource des informations
es fleurs et des plantes.

Plantes

A

ANIMALS

Cows Caught in the Web

Cow sounds, portraits, trivia and moooch mooore.

URL http://www.brandonu.ca/~ennsnr/
Cows/Welcome.html

Electronic Zoo

All of the fun without the hair and that peculiar smell.

URL http://netvet.wustl.edu/
e-zoo.htm

FINS

The Fish Information Service provides information about aquariums.

URL http://www.actwin.com/fish

Fish Cam

Netscape displays a constantly updating picture of their office fish tank.

URL http://home.netscape.com/
fishcam

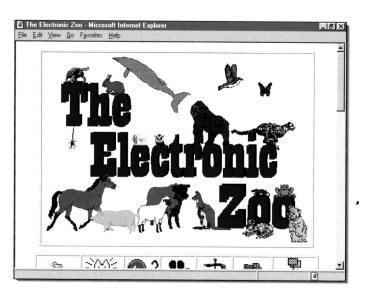

Horse Country

Lots of pictures and information on horses and horseback riding are stored at this site.

URL http://www.horse-country.com

NetPets

Order pet supplies on the Web or look at a database of dog breeds and other pet information.

URL http://www.netpets.com

NetVet Veterinary Resources

A great place to find veterinary and animal resources.

URL http://netvet.wustl.edu

Online Book of Parrots

This virtual book on parrots and parrot-like birds cannot be imitated.

URL http://www.ub.tu-clausthal.de/
p_welcome.html

Pet Shoppe

Order from a huge catalog of items for all sorts of pets.

URL http://www.petshoppe.com

Tennessee Aquarium

Take a tour of the world's largest freshwater aquarium.

URL http://www.tennis.org

Turtle Trax

Information on marine turtles and what you can do to help them.

URL http://www.turtles.org

Virtual Pet Cemetery

This site allows people to post small obituaries of their lost pets.

URL http://www.lavamind.com/pet.html

A Page Devoted to Marine Turtles

Aloha, and thanks for stopping by.

Turtle Trax contains numerous images, but please don't let that intimidate you. We've tried to keep it friendly to text browsers as well, and to make it informative even without the graphics.

ART

African Art Exhibit

This site exhibits African art and describes African culture.

URL http://www.lib.virginia.edu/dic/exhib/ 93.ray.aa/African.html

Andy Warhol

This site offers information on The Andy Warhol Museum in Pittsburgh, PA.

URL http://www.warhol.org/warhol

Art of Tibetan Sand Painting

Check out the pictures and movies documenting the creation of a sand painting by Tibetan monks.

URL http://www.chron.com/mandala

Art on the Net

Artists, writers and musicians from around the world use this site to share their work.

URL http://www.art.net

Body Modification Ezine

That's right — body piercing and tattooing are now known as Body Art.

URL http://bme.freeq.com

Electric Gallery

This site offers many paintings that you can view and even buy if you like.

URL http://www.egallery.com/index.html

Kaleidospace

This site offers a wide variety of work from independent artists.

URL http://kspace.com

Leonardo da Vinci

You can view many works by the famous artist and engineer.

URL http://www.leonardo.net/main.html

Museum of Bad Art

The place for art too bad to be ignored.

URL http://glyphs.com/moba

National Museum of American Art

View almost 1,000 works of art from across the United States.

URL http://www.nmaa.si.edu

Rock & Roll Digital Gallery

Check this site frequently to view the latest exhibition of rock and roll artwork.

URL http://www.hooked.net/julianne/
index.html

The Café

More than an art gallery, this is a cyber-hangout where you can look at art, watch movies, chat with other art lovers or read some great poetry.

URL http://www.virtualcafe.com

Time Life Photo Sight

A collection of photographs from Time's archives.

URL http://www.pathfinder.com/pathfinder/photo/sighthome.html

WebMuseum

You can view works of art by some of the most famous painters in the world, including Michelangelo, Renoir, Monet and Picasso.

URL http://www.emf.net/louvre

ASTRONOMY

Bradford Robotic Telescope Observatory Site

This great guide to the universe is taken from a multimedia CD-ROM.

URL http://www.eia.brad.ac.uk/btl

Internet UFO Group

This site lets you read articles and catch up on the latest UFO sightings.

URL http://www.iufog.org

NASA

NASA presents pictures, information and links to all major NASA research locations in the U.S.

URL http://www.nasa.gov

National Space Science Data Center

This site contains a photo gallery and various space-related information.

URL http://nssdc.gsfc.nasa.gov

Shuttle Web

NASA's status report keeps you up-to-date on the space shuttle.

URL http://shuttle.nasa.gov

Views of the Solar System

Travel light years away with the click of your mouse.

URL http://bang.lanl.gov/solarsys

B

BIOLOGY

Bio Online

One of the top sites for information on biotechnology.

URL http://www.bio.com

Biosciences

A guide to biology on the Internet.

URL http://golgi.harvard.edu/
biopages/all.html

Cell Online

A collection of biology journals.

URL http://www.cell.com

Dictionary of Cell Biology

You can find those important definitions for your next biology essay.

URL http://www.mblab.gla.ac.uk/
~julian/Dict.html

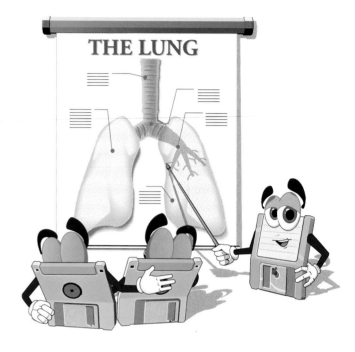

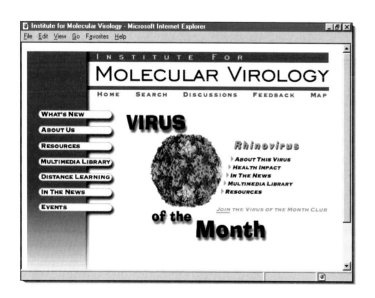

Entomology

Colorado State's collection of bug information.

URL http://www.colostate.edu/Depts/
Entomology/ent.html

Institute for Molecular Virology

Articles, pictures and information concerning various viruses.

URL http://www.bocklabs.wisc.edu/
Welcome.html

Pharmaceutical Information Network

If you want information on prescription drugs or on pharmacies in general, look here.

URL http://pharminfo.com

USGS Biology

A directory of biological science sites on the Web.

URL http://info.er.usgs.gov/network/
science/biology/index.html

BIZARRE

Anagram Insanity

Give this Web page a phrase and it will use the letters to make another sentence.

URL http://Infobahn.COM:80/pages/ anagram.html

Blue Dog

A dog will bark the correct answer to a math question you ask.

URL http://kao.ini.cmu.edu:5550/ bdf.html

Britannica's Lives

Find out which famous people were born today.

URL http://www.eb.com/cgi-bin/ bio.pl

Captain Kirk Sing-a-long Page

William Shatner croons his heart out on this quirky page.

URL http://www.loskene.com/ singalong/kirk.html

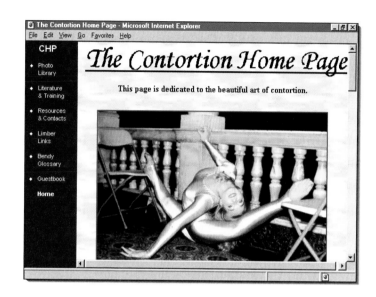

Carlos' Coloring Book

Color a picture of anything from an apple to a leprechaun at this site.

URL http://www.ravenna.com/coloring

Chia Pet Zoo

A humorous, photographic tribute to Chia Pets.

URL http://www.accessone.com/~jonathin

Church of the SubGenius

Let Bob guide you down the true path of Slack.

URL http://sunsite.unc.edu/subgenius

Contortion Home Page

A page dedicated to some very flexible individuals.

URL http://www.escape.com/~silverbk/ contortion

B

Land O' Useless Facts

Get a daily dose of useless trivia or browse through the extensive archives of useless facts.

URL http://www-leland.stanford.edu/
~jenkg/useless.html

Monkeys Typing Shakespeare

See if this virtual monkey can actually manage to type "to be or not to be, that is the question."

URL http://bronte.cs.utas.edu.au/monkey

Mr. Edible Starchy Tuber Head

An online toy that just happens to look like the Mr. Potatohead doll.

URL http://winnie.acsu.buffalo.edu/
potatoe

Plastic Princess Collector's Page

A great place for barbie doll collectors. This site includes information on doll shows, price guides and links to other Web sites.

URL http://d.armory.com/~zenugirl/
barbie.html

Send a Virtual Postcard

Send a postcard to someone else on the Internet via this site at MIT.

URL http://postcards.www.media.mit.edu/
Postcards

The Spot

Live vicariously through six online teenagers.

URL http://www.thespot.com

Top Tips

The place to go if you want silly tips on doing just about anything.

URL http://www.emtex.com/toptips

T.W.I.N.K.I.E.S.

Tests With Inorganic Noxious Kakes In Extreme Situations. That's right, you can watch Twinkies blow up into a million pieces.

URL http://www.owlnet.rice.edu/
~gouge/twinkies.html

Virtual Confession Booth

Your chance to confess your sins from the comfort of your home.

URL http://anther.learning.cs.cmu. edu/priest.html

BOOKS AND LANGUAGE

A-ha! Books

Order from a daily updated catalog of rare and out-of-print books.

URL http://www.lightlink.com/tokman

Amazon.com

The Internet's largest bookstore, with over two million books for sale.

URL http://www.amazon.com

AudioBooks

A catalog of books on tape.

URL http://www.audiobooks.com

Bantam Doubleday Dell

One of North America's largest publishers has information on their books and a daily puzzle.

URL http://www.bdd.com

Book Stacks

Another of the Internet's major online book stores.

URL http://www.books.com

BookWire

A good place to start if you're looking for book information.

URL http://www.bookwire.com

Children's Literature

A guide to books for the little ones.

URL http://www.ucalgary.ca/~dkbrown/ index.html

B

Elementary Grammar

Remember—I before E, except after C. This site offers grammar lessons.

URL http://www.hiway.co.uk/~ei/intro.html

English Server

Carnegie Mellon University uses this site to distribute research, novels, criticism and much more.

URL http://english-www.hss.cmu.edu

IDG Books

IDG publishes the Dummies series, the 3-D Visual series and many others.

URL http://www.idgbooks.com

Internet Public Library

Many reference books are available here, including a thesaurus and dictionary.

URL http://ipl.sils.umich.edu

Library of Congress

You can't read the books online, but you can search for one of interest.

URL http://lcweb.loc.gov/homepage/lchp.html

maranGraphics

Find out more about the world's most user-friendly computer books.

URL http://www.maran.com

On-line Books

A collection of books at Carnegie Mellon University.

URL http://www.cs.cmu.edu/Web/books.html

Shakespeare Web

A good place to start if you want to learn more about Shakespeare.

URL http://www.shakespeare.com

Virtual Reference Desk

Use a thesaurus, dictionary or phone book here.

URL http://thorplus.lib.purdue.edu/reference/index.html

BUSINESS: COMPANIES

American Airlines

Browse through airline schedules, fares and much more.

URL http://www.americanair.com

AT&T

This site offers a wide variety of telecommunications services.

URL http://www.att.com

Best Western International

At this site you can view hotel information and make reservations online at any Best Western hotel in the world.

URL http://www.bestwestern.com/best.html

Canadian Airlines

Browse through airline schedules, inflight movies, special meals and much more.

URL http://www.CdnAir.ca

Crayola

This site tells you how crayons are made and the colors the company produces.

URL http://www.crayola.com/crayola

FAO Schwarz

More toys than you can imagine.

URL http://faoschwarz.com

FedEx

Track your package online and make sure it arrives safely.

URL http://www.fedex.com

B

Guess

Go behind the scenes at a Guess photo-shoot or send a digital postcard to a friend.

URL http://www.guess.com

JCPenney

This chain of department stores lets you browse through their products from the comfort of your own home.

URL http://www.jcpenney.com

Joe Boxer

This site is less about underwear and more about having fun.

URL http://www.joeboxer.com

Kodak

This site offers a great collection of digital images.

URL http://www.kodak.com

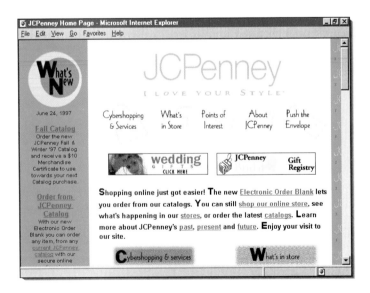

L'eggs Pantyhose

You can buy pantyhose online at this site.

URL http://www.pantyhose.com

Magnavox

You can find information on the company, its products and electronics in general.

URL http://www.magnavox.com

Molson

Information on Molson and its products.

URL http://www.molson.com

Neiman Marcus

Get the latest news from the fashion world or find out what is happening at Neiman Marcus this month.

URL http://www.neimanmarcus.com

Pepsi

Hang around Pepsi World and win fabulous prizes!

URL http://www.pepsi.com

Ragu

This is a top-notch site with recipes, contests and guides to speaking Italian.

URL http://www.eat.com

Sprint

Find out all about the long distance company at this site.

URL http://www.sprint.com

TicketMaster

Look up events, read interviews and win free concert tickets!

URL U.S.   http://www.ticketmaster.com
URL Canada   http://www.ticketmaster.ca

Time Warner Inc.

All the news, sports and entertainment information you could ask for.

URL http://www.pathfinder.com

UPS

Use the United Parcel Service site to track your package across the country.

URL http://www.ups.com

Virtual Vineyards

Read about wine at this site or buy your favorite bottle.

URL http://www.virtualvin.com

Wal-Mart

The management team's quote of the day and much more.

URL http://www.wal-mart.com

B

BUSINESS: FINANCE

American Stock Exchange

Check today's market summary or look back through the archives for the past year.

URL http://www.amex.com

BarterWire

Don't pay cash—barter for it!

URL http://www.itex.net

Citibank

One of the largest banks in the U.S.

URL http://www.citicorp.com

Coin Universe

Resources for collectors, dealers and anyone else interested in coins from around the world.

URL http://www.coin-universe.com/index.html

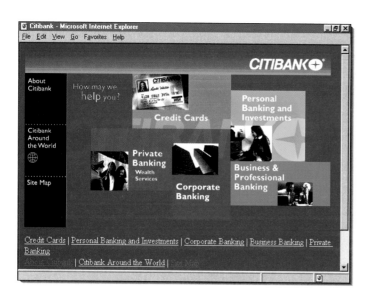

Finance on the WWW

This site in Denmark is filled with links to business and finance.

URL http://www.wiso.gwdg.de/ifbg/finance.html

Money and Investing Update

The Wall Street Journal's financial news page.

URL http://update.wsj.com

Money Magazine

A great source of financial information, from loan rates to investment ideas.

URL http://www.pathfinder.com/money

Mutual Funds Home Page

Get advice from the experts before you part with your hard-earned cash.

URL http://www.brill.com

Online Banking & Financial Services Directory

Yet another list of money-related sites on the Web.

URL http://www.orcc.com/orcc/banking.htm

PCQuote

A great place to get delayed stock quotes free of charge.

URL http://www.pcquote.com

Principal Financial Group

The place to look for information on retirement plans, mutual funds, life insurance and many other investment ideas.

URL http://www.principal.com

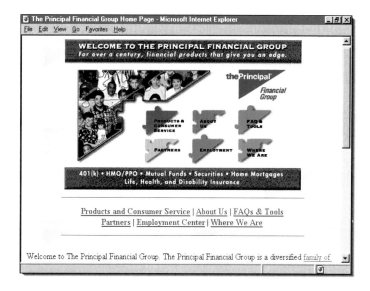

Security APL

Security APL provides stock quotes to the public.

URL http://www.secapl.com

Stock Master

Check out which mutual funds are hot and whichfunds are not.

URL http://www.stockmaster.com

USA Today - Money

Read about what's new in the financial world.

URL http://www.usatoday.com/money/mfront.htm

Wells Fargo

The oldest bank in the West has a wide variety of services on the Internet.

URL http://www.wellsfargo.com

World Bank

Find out all about the World Bank at this site.

URL http://www.worldbank.org

BC

BUSINESS: SHOPPING

Access Market Square

You can find many unique products and gifts at this site.

URL http://www.icw.com/ams.html

Catalog Mart

The easiest and fastest way to get just about any catalog available in the U.S. Choose from more than 10,000 - all free!

URL http://catalog.savvy.com

CommerceNet

This site provides an index of commercial products and services available on the Internet.

URL http://www.commerce.net

eMall

Products, services and information— this site has something for everyone.

URL http://eMall.com

Fingerhut Online

Fingerhut offers a wide variety of products including jewelry, electronics, clothing and much more.

URL http://www.fingerhut.com

imall

This site offers links to other products and services on the Internet.

URL http://www.imall.com

Internet Mall

Find out where you can purchase food, clothing, furniture, gifts and much more.

URL http://www.internet-mall.com

Internet Shopping Network

A site with hot deals and Internet specials.

URL http://www.internet.net

Malls of Canada

Canada's largest Internet shopping mall offers goods and services from across Canada.

URL http://www.canadamalls.com/provider

NECX

Over 30,000 computer products are available here.

URL http://www.necx.com

ParentsPlace

Everything for parents and children—books, diapers, toys and more.

URL http://www.parentsplace.com/
shopping/index.html

Shop at Home

Search by name, keyword or category for a catalog of interest.

URL http://www.shopathome.com

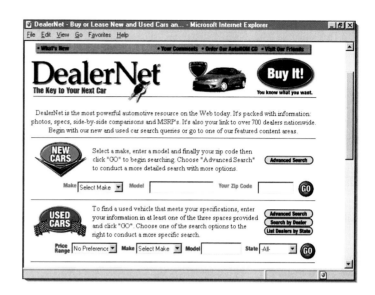

Cars

Alamo Rent A Car

Reserve a car online and check out the weather for where you are headed.

URL http://www.freeways.com

AutoWeb

Advertised as "The Internet's Premier Auto Mall."

URL http://www.autoweb.com

Cadillac

You can find information on the new Cadillacs or check out upcoming Cadillac-sponsored events.

URL http://www.cadillac.com

DealerNet

A great place to look for information on a variety of vehicles.

URL http://www.dealernet.com

Ford

All the Ford information your heart desires.

URL http://www.ford.com

General Motors

A comprehensive site from the world's largest car maker.

URL http://www.gm.com

Goodyear

They've got lots of tires and a very big blimp.

URL http://www.goodyear.com

Harley Davidson Motorcycles of Stamford

Okay, so it's not a car—it still has wheels.

URL http://www.hd-stamford.com

Honda

Honda in America, with a timeline, monthly specials, a virtual plant tour and more.

URL http://www.honda.com

Jeep

For those who crave the rugged outdoors.

URL http://www.jeepunpaved.com

Nissan Motors

Explore the world of Nissan in four languages or go on the Pathfinder African Adventure.

URL http://www.nissanmotors.com

Saturn

This site is geared towards Saturn owners, but prospective buyers should also check it out.

URL http://www.saturncars.com

Toyota

You can find information on Toyota's vehicles, dealers and much more.

URL http://www.toyota.com

Volvo

Check out the new line of Volvos or locate the dealer nearest you.

URL http://www.volvocars.com

CHEMISTRY

Chemistry Hypermedia Project

Provides resources and educational material for chemistry students.

URL http://www.chem.vt.edu/chem-ed/
vt-chem-ed.html

Chemistry Virtual Library

This site provides links to chemistry departments around the world.

URL http://www.chem.ucla.edu/
chempointers.html

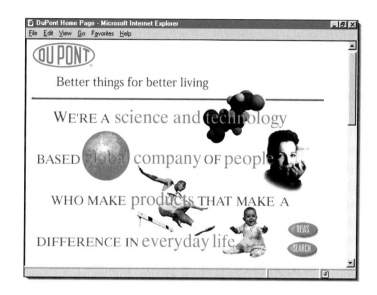

Chemist's Art Gallery

Pictures and animations of molecules and other aspects of chemistry.

URL http://www.csc.fi/lul/chem/graphics.html

DuPont

One of North America's largest chemical companies.

URL http://www.dupont.com

Ethics in Science

The rights and wrongs of chemistry and science in general.

URL http://www.chem.vt.edu/ethics/ethics.html

Internet Chemistry Index

A list of chemistry FTP, Gopher and WWW sites on the Internet.

URL http://www.chemie.fu-berlin.de/
chemistry/index

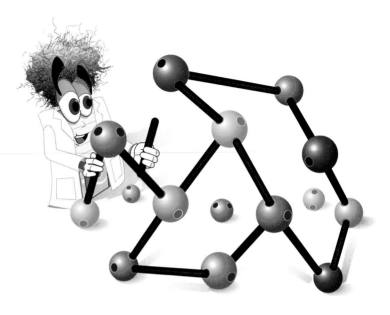

Internet Chemistry Resources

This site provides links to other chemistry sites and gives you access to databases, catalogs and much more.

URL http://www.rpi.edu/dept/chem/ cheminfo/chemres.html

National Academy of Sciences

A list of scientific committees and resources across the U.S.

URL http://www.nas.edu

Periodic Table of the Elements

Click on an element in the Periodic Table to get information about that element.

URL http://mwanal.lanl.gov/CST/ imagemap/periodic/periodic.html

Royal Society of Chemistry

This site is for students, teachers or anyone interested in chemistry.

URL http://chemistry.rsc.org/rsc

Wilson Group

This chemistry research site will help you visualize molecules.

URL http://www-wilson.ucsd.edu

COMPUTERS: PICTURES

Clip Art Connection

More than 2,000 samples of clip art as well as links to other sites, including a site with information on how to use clip art at home.

URL http://www.ist.net/clipart/index.html

Cool Science Image

Lots of incredibly cool pictures of insects, plants, planets and more.

URL http://whyfiles.news.wisc.edu/ coolimages

John Donohue's National Park Photos

Excellent photos of America's best national parks.

URL http://www.panix.com/~wizjd/ parks/parks.html

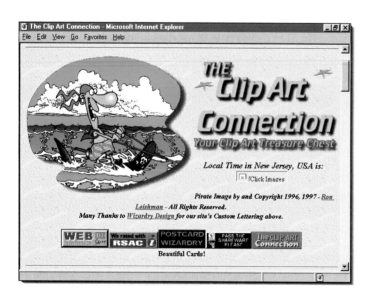

Kite Site

Pictures of all sorts of kites.

URL http://www.latrobe.edu.au/Glenn/
KiteSite/Kites.html

Lighthouses

Pictures of lighthouses from around
the world.

URL http://www.ipl.org/exhibit/light

Michigan Press Photographers Association

Browse through the winning photos in
the Pictures of the Year contest.

URL http://www.mppa.org

NSSDC Photo Gallery

The National Space Science Data
Center has pictures of planets,
asteroids and more.

URL http://nssdc.gsfc.nasa.gov/
photo_gallery

Photo Exhibitions and Archives

A list of photo exhibits on the Web.

URL http://www.algonet.se/~bengtha/
photo/exhibits.html

SunSite Archive

A huge list of pictures sorted into categories.

URL http://sunsite.unc.edu/pub/
multimedia/pictures

Swedish FTP Archive

Pictures of almost anything you can imagine.

URL http://ftp.sunet.se/pub/pictures

Time Life Photo Sight

The best of Time Life's large collection of photos.

URL http://www.pathfinder.com/
pathfinder/photo/sighthome.html

ZooNet Archive

Pictures of all the animals you would find in a zoo.

URL http://www.mindspring.com/
~zoonet/gallery.html

COMPUTERS: RESOURCES

Adobe

The creators of Photoshop, Illustrator and other graphics programs.

URL http://www.adobe.com

Apple Computer

The Macintosh home page informs users about the latest news at Apple.

URL http://www.apple.com

Borland

Borland creates database and programming software.

URL http://www.borland.com

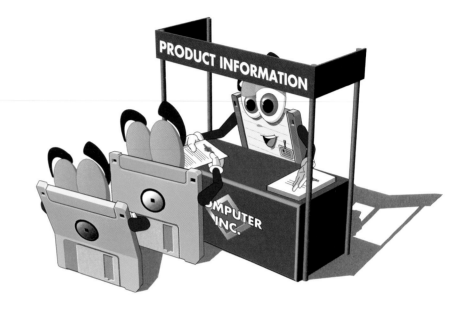

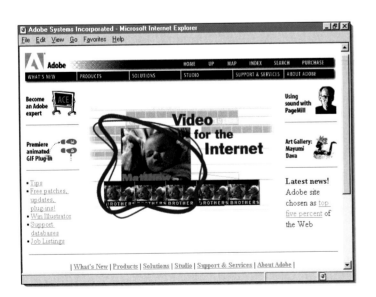

Compaq

One of North America's largest manufacturers of personal computers.

URL http://www.compaq.com/

Computer Museum

Find interactive exhibits, the history of computing and more at this site.

URL http://www.net.org/

Dell

One of Compaq's biggest competitors.

URL http://www.dell.com/

Hewlett-Packard

One of the top manufacturers of printers, computers and scanners.

URL http://www.hp.com/

IBM

The giant computer conglomerate known as "Big Blue."

URL http://www.ibm.com

Intel

Intel creates the main processor used in most personal computers.

URL http://www.intel.com

Internet Phone

With a microphone, sound card, speakers and the Internet Phone program, you can say good-bye to long-distance telephone charges.

URL http://www.vocaltec.com

Java Tutorial

A guide to Java, the programming language used on the Internet.

URL http://java.sun.com/nav/read/Tutorial/index.html

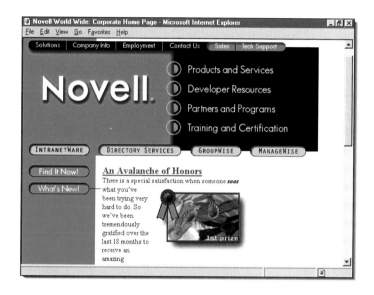

McAfee

One of the leading manufacturers of virus-protection software.

URL http://www.mcafee.com

Microsoft

This computer software giant has landed on the Web.

URL http://www.microsoft.com

NCSA at UIUC

The National Center for Supercomputing Applications created NCSA Mosaic, the first graphical Web browser.

URL http://www.ncsa.uiuc.edu/

Novell

Novell software runs many networks around the world.

URL http://www.novell.com

Silicon Graphics

Known for their high-end computers and for WebSpace, their VRML browser.

URL http://www.sgi.com/

TUCOWS

The Ultimate Collection of Windows Software that helps PCs use the Internet.

URL http://www.tucows.com

COMPUTERS: SOUNDS

Blue Dog

A dog will bark the correct answer to a math question you ask.

URL http://kao.ini.cmu.edu:5550/
bdf.html

Creative Zone

Makers of the ever-popular Sound Blaster sound card.

URL http://www.creaf.com/

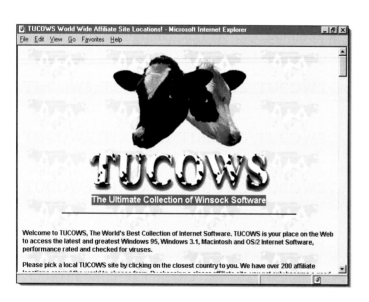

Historical Speeches

Listen to speeches by Richard Nixon, JFK and many others.

URL http://www.webcorp.com/sounds/
index.htm

Internet Underground Music Archive

A cool place to hear independent artists and bands.

URL http://www.iuma.com/

Japanese Sound Archive

The sounds have nothing to do with Japan, but this site is large and fast.

URL http://sunsite.sut.ac.jp/multimed/sounds/

John Lennon Sound Files

This site has become very popular because you can download previously unreleased songs to your computer.

URL http://www.bagism.com

Movie Sounds

Sounds from all of your favorite movies.

URL http://www.moviesounds.com

PolyGram Records

This site features sound and video clips as well as a diverse collection of artists such as Def Leppard and ABBA.

URL http://www.polygram.com/polygram/
Music.html

RealAudio

Hear sound instantly, without delay!

URL http://www.realaudio.com

Sony Music

Artist information, tour dates and a collection of sound and video recordings of your favorite artists can be found here.

URL http://www.music.sony.com/Music/
MusicIndex.html

SunSite Sounds

You can find songs, quotes and more at this large sound collection.

URL http://sunsite.unc.edu/pub/multimedia/
pc-sounds

Text to Speech

Type something and this Web site will actually say it back!

URL http://wwwtios.cs.utwente.nl/say

Vincent Voice Library

A selection of historical speeches and lectures.

URL http://web.msu.edu/vincent/index.html

Warsaw University

Warsaw is one of many universities around the world that have collections of sound.

URL http://info.fuw.edu.pl/multimedia/sounds

DE

DANCE AND DANCE MUSIC

Belly Dance Home Page

An entire Web site dedicated to the art of belly dancing.

URL http://cie-2.uoregon.edu/bdance

Breaks

A site dedicated to breakbeat music.

URL http://www.breaks.com

CyberDance-Ballet on the Net

A great source for links to ballet and modern dance information on the Internet.

URL http://www.thepoint.net/~raw/dance.htm

Dancescape

Your guide to the world of ballroom dancing.

URL http://wchat.on.ca/dance/pages/dscape1.htm

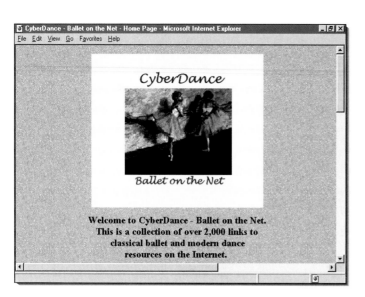

Dance Online

You will find information on performances, reviews and links to other Web sites.

URL http://www.danceonline.com

Ernesto's Tango Page

Put a rose between your teeth before you visit this site.

URL http://www.ims.uni-stuttgart.de/phonetik/ernst/tango/ebtango.html

Henry's Dance Hotlist

An Internet user named Henry has a list of sites about different types of dancing.

URL http://zeus.ncsa.uiuc.edu:8080/~hneeman/dance_hotlist.html

Hyperreal

A collection of rave culture and music resources.

URL http://www.hyperreal.com

Information Super Dance Floor

A great resource for those who want to learn the latest country music dance steps.

URL http://www.apci.net/~drdeyne

Let's Dance

You can flip through an online catalog for all your dancewear needs.

URL http://letsdance.com

National Ballet of Canada

News and information about the company's upcoming shows and ticket prices.

URL http://www.ffa.ucalgary.ca/nbc/ nbc_main.html

Square and Round Dance Page

Interested in square or round dancing? This site will tell you which clubs to visit and much more.

URL http://pages.prodigy.com/sq.dance

Streetsound

A site designed for dance music DJs and fans.

URL http://www.streetsound.com/zone

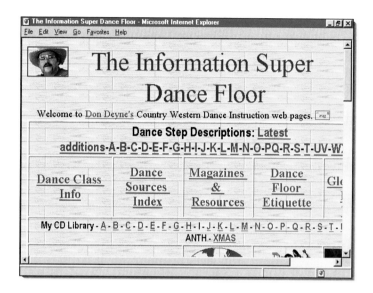

VIBE Magazine Online

The online version of VIBE, the dance music magazine.

URL http://www.pathfinder.com/vibe

E DUCATION

AskERIC

This service is well-known for its resources for teachers.

URL http://ericir.syr.edu

CollegeNET

A searchable database of over 2,000 universities and colleges.

URL http://www.collegenet.com

E

EdLinks

Links to educational sites of every size and shape.

URL http://webpages.marshall.edu/~jmullens/edlinks.html

EdWeb

Find out about technology and school reform at this site.

URL http://k12.cnidr.org:90

fastWEB

A guide to finding university and college scholarships.

URL http://www.studentservices.com/fastweb

Frank Potter's Science Gems

A collection of science and mathematics resources available on the Web.

URL http://www-sci.lib.uci.edu/SEP/SEP.html

Global SchoolNet Foundation

This site is dedicated to linking kids around the world and offers projects, contests and much more.

URL http://gsn.org

Global Show-n-Tell

Kids can show their stuff to other kids around the world.

URL http://www.telenaut.com/gst/

Kidlink

This site offers several different forums that allow 10- to 15-year-old students around the world to communicate.

URL http://www.kidlink.org

KidPub

Where kids and classes can post their stories and poems.

URL http://www.kidpub.org/kidpub

Kids' Space

A fantastic place for kids to share their imaginations with other kids.

URL http://www.kids-space.org

Media Literacy Online Project

A collection of information about the influence of the media in our lives.

URL http://interact.uoregon.edu/MediaLit/HomePage

Online Educational Resources

A collection of educational resources for students and teachers.

URL http://quest.arc.nasa.gov/OER

Teaching and Learning on the Web

This site is for more than just net surfing—you can search for sites of interest here.

URL http://www.mcli.dist.maricopa.edu/tl/

Yale University

Find out about programs and campus life at Yale.

URL http://www.yale.edu

ENVIRONMENT AND WEATHER

Daily Planet

This site has links to several weather resources on the World Wide Web.

URL http://www.atmos.uiuc.edu

EcoNet

EcoNet has several sister networks, including PeaceNet, LaborNet and WomensNet.

URL http://www.igc.apc.org/econet

EnviroLink Network

The largest online source of environmental information.

URL http://envirolink.org

Environmental Protection Agency

Learn how the government is making a difference.

URL http://www.epa.gov

Greenpeace

While you can't race alongside an oil tanker online, this WWW site gives you a taste of Greenpeace.

URL http://www.greenpeace.org

INTELLiCast

Check out the weather around the world.

URL http://www.intellicast.com

Internet Disaster Information Network

Information on the latest disasters around the world.

URL http://www.disaster.net/index.html

National Oceanic and Atmospheric Administration

Find out what the U.S. government is doing about the ozone layer, endangered species and more.

URL http://www.noaa.gov

Rainforest Action Network

This beautiful site promotes the preservation of the Earth's rainforests.

URL http://www.ran.org/ran

Recycler's World

A site dedicated to recycling.

URL http://www.sentex.net/recycle

Science and the Environment

Topics at this site include clean air and water, recycling, health, population, agriculture, alternative energy and more.

URL http://www.cais.net/publish/
stories/allstory.htm

USA Today Weather

Weather information from one of the largest newspapers in the U.S.

URL http://www.usatoday.com/weather/
wfront.htm

Weather Information Superhighway

This site offers links to many weather-related Web pages.

URL http://www.nws.fsu.edu/wxhwy.html

WeatherNet: Weather Cams

Spy on the weather with current weather pictures taken from cameras mounted in a variety of locations all over the U.S. and Canada.

URL http://cirrus.sprl.umich.edu/wxnet/wxcam.html

FOOD AND DRINK

Beer Page

This site provides information and recipes for homebrewers.

URL http://www.realbeer.com/spencer

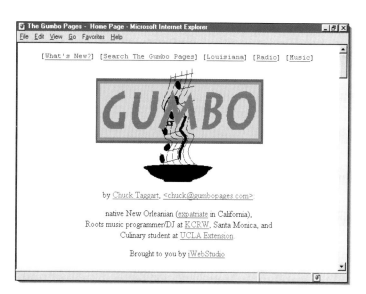

Coca-Cola

This site has information on the company and its products, as well as little things to amuse you.

URL http://www.cocacola.com

Godiva Chocolates

This site includes recipes and a Godiva catalog you can look through.

URL http://www.godiva.com

Gumbo Pages

You can find information on the food, music and culture of New Orleans.

URL http://www.gumbopages.com

Hershey Foods Corporation

The company known for its chocolate kisses.

URL http://www.microserve.net/~hershey/welcome.html

Ketchum Kitchen

Recipes, discussions and much more.

URL http://www.recipe.com

Mentos

Links to the Mentos art gallery and a neat list of frequently asked questions.

URL http://www.mentos.com

Pasta Home Page

Pasta lovers, this is your site! Find recipes, answers to popular questions and information on nutrition and pasta shapes.

URL http://www.ilovepasta.org

Perrier

This site has contests, a gallery of art bottles and much more.

URL http://www.perrier.com

Recipe Archive

Learn to make everything from lasagna to cheesecake at this site.

URL http://www.vuw.ac.nz/~amyl/recipes

Rubbermaid

Find information on the products that keep your food fresh!

URL http://www.rubbermaid.com

Star Chefs

Get recipes and tips from great chefs and cookbook authors.

URL http://starchefs.com

Vegetarian Pages

News, recipes, a list of famous vegetarians and much more.

URL http://www.veg.org/veg

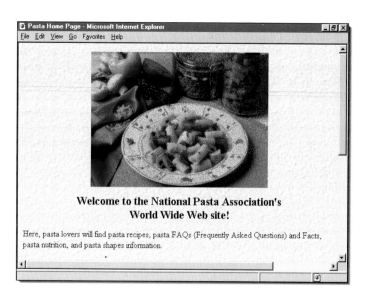

Welcome to the National Pasta Association's World Wide Web site!

Here, pasta lovers will find pasta recipes, pasta FAQs (Frequently Asked Questions) and Facts, pasta nutrition, and pasta shapes information.

AMES

Dogz

Get a free demo of a pet dog that lives on your computer desktop.

URL http://fido.dogz.com/dogz

Duck Hunt

Find the ducks hidden at this site.

URL http://aurora.york.ac.uk/ducks.html

Electronic Arts

One of the top game-makers in North America.

URL http://www.ea.com

Games Domain

This popular site offers free games and tips on some of the most popular computer games on the market.

URL http://www.gamesdomain.com

Happy Puppy

A huge collection of games, demos, strategy tips and more.

URL http://happypuppy.com

Jumbo

A collection of free programs for DOS, Windows and Macintosh computers.

URL http://www.jumbo.com

LucasArts

Creators of many top-rated computer games like Full Throttle and Dark Forces.

URL http://www.lucasarts.com/menu.html

Madlib

This site creates a wacky story based on a few words you enter.

URL http://www.ii.uib.no/~tor/cgi/madlib.html

Maxis

This company has produced the popular simulation series that includes SimCity, SimCity 2000, SimEarth and SimAnt.

URL http://www.maxis.com

NEXT Generation

The online version of the magazine that provides the latest information on games and the game industry.

URL http://www.next-generation.com

Nintendo Power Source

Nintendo offers information on its products and links to other cool sites you can visit.

URL http://www.nintendo.com

PC Gamer Online

Find reviews, previews and gaming news at the online outpost of this computer gaming magazine.

URL http://www.pcgamer.com

Riddler

Solve puzzles and riddles for cash and prizes.

URL http://www.riddler.com

Sega Online

Find out more about Genesis, Game Gear and Saturn from this video game giant.

URL http://www.sega.com

Shareware.com

This powerful tool helps you find programs that you can copy to your computer.

URL http://www.shareware.com

Virtual Vegas

Virtual Vegas has blackjack, poker, roulette and more for the gambler in you.

URL http://www.virtualvegas.com

GEOGRAPHY

CityNet

One of the most popular sites on the Internet, CityNet provides information on most major cities worldwide.

URL http://city.net

How far is it?

Enter two places and this Web site will tell you the distance between them.

URL http://www.indo.com/distance

Map Viewer

This site offers maps of the world and plans to add more features in the future.

URL http://pubweb.parc.xerox.com/map

Mt. Rushmore Home Page

Don't you just wish your face was up there too?

URL http://www.state.sd.us./state/executive/
tourism/rushmore/rushmore.html

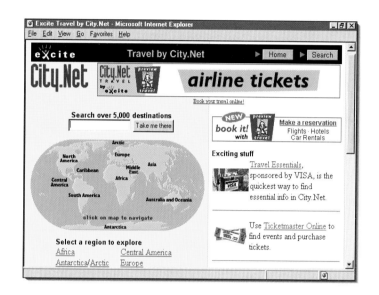

National Climatic Data Center

Find out where it's hot and where it's not.

URL http://www.ncdc.noaa.gov

NCGIA

Find out about the National Center for Geographic Information and Analysis.

URL http://www.ncgia.ucsb.edu

PCL Map Collection

The mother of all map collections.

URL http://www.lib.utexas.edu/Libs/PCL/
Map_collection/Map_collection.html

U.S. Geological Survey

This site provides information to help you better understand earth sciences.

URL http://www.usgs.gov

G

GOVERNMENT AND INFORMATION ON THE U.S.

Air Force
This site lets you access most U.S. Air Force bases nationwide.

URL http://w3.af.mil

Army
You can flip through Soldiers, an online magazine, visit other army-related sites and much more.

URL http://www.army.mil

Census Bureau
Find out how many people are currently living in the U.S.

URL http://www.census.gov

CIA
This is a public site, so you won't find the government's deepest, darkest secrets here.

URL http://www.odci.gov/cia

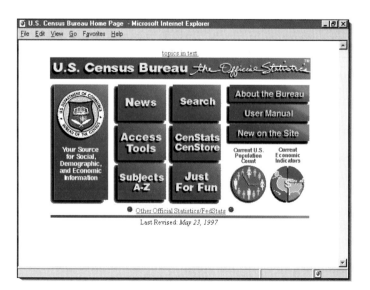

Coast Guard
This isn't Baywatch.

URL http://www.webcom.com/~d13www/welcome.html

DefenseLINK
The U.S. Defense Department's online handbook.

URL http://www.dtic.dla.mil/defenselink

Department of Education
This site provides information for both students and teachers.

URL http://www.ed.gov

Department of Justice
They fight to protect your rights. This site has links to many agencies, including the FBI.

URL http://www.usdoj.gov

Department of the Treasury

The people who make all our coins. This site provides information on the programs and activities of the Department of the Treasury.

URL http://www.ustreas.gov

FBI

Find out about the FBI and keep up-to-date on the latest investigations.

URL http://www.fbi.gov

Federal Budget

Find out where all your money is going.

URL http://ibert.org

Federal Courts' Home Page

A great source for information regarding the Judicial Branch of the U.S. Government.

URL http://www.uscourts.gov

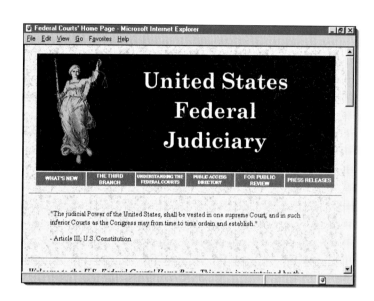

Forest Service

This is the site that Smokey the Bear calls home.

URL http://www.fs.fed.us.

House of Representatives

This site provides information on legislation, committees and organizations of the House.

URL http://www.house.gov

Library of Congress

While you can't read many of the books, you can search for details on almost any publication in North America.

URL http://lcweb.loc.gov

NavyOnLine

The complete guide to the U.S. Navy.

URL http://www.navy.mil

New York State

The Empire State goes online!

URL http://www.state.ny.us

Postal Service

Look up a zip code, find a postage rate and much more here.

URL http://www.usps.gov

Thomas Library

This immense site has a great deal of congressional and legislative information.

URL http://thomas.loc.gov

White House

See the First Family or take a tour of the White House.

URL http://www.whitehouse.gov

United Kingdom

Saudi Arabia

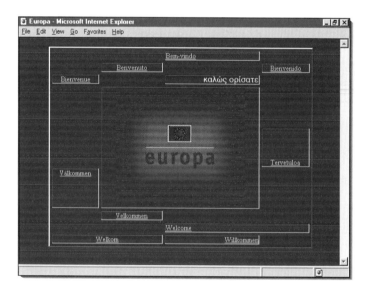

GOVERNMENTS AND INFORMATION ON THE WORLD

Australian Government

Information on the government of the Land Down Under.

URL http://gov.info.au

Europa Home Page

This site offers information on the European Union's goals and policies.

URL http://europa.eu.int/index.htm

Hong Kong Government Information Center

Pictures, government offices, news updates and a lot more on Hong Kong.

URL http://www.info.gov.hk

New Zealand

Learn all there is to know about this country in the Pacific.

URL http://www.akiko.lm.com/nz

URL http://www.akiko.lm.com

Russia Today

Take a look at what is happening in Russia today with this site's thorough coverage of Russian politics.

URL http://www.russiatoday.com

Saudi Arabia

An intriguing look at the Middle Eastern country.

URL http://imedl.saudi.net

South African Government of National Unity

Visit this site to learn more about the new, democratic South Africa.

URL http://www.polity.org.za/gnu

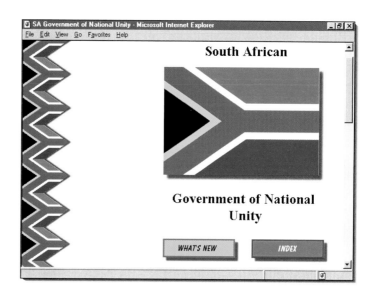

United Kingdom

This site helps you locate government offices, services and officials in the United Kingdom.

URL http://www.open.gov.uk

United Nations

Take a tour of the U.N. or keep up-to-date with the latest information on international relations.

URL http://www.un.org

World Bank

Find out all about the World Bank Group here.

URL http://www.worldbank.org

HEALTH

Acupuncture Home Page

If you do not like needles, point your Web browser in another direction.

URL http://www.rscom.com/tcm/index.htm

American Medical Association

You can find medical journals and much more at this site.

URL http://www.ama-assn.org

Centers for Disease Control

Learn how to prevent and control many diseases, injuries and disabilities.

URL http://www.cdc.gov

Central Institute for the Deaf

This site provides information on the Institute's programs and education for the hearing impaired.

URL http://cidmac.wustl.edu

Cyber Pharmacy

A pharmacy that provides online information and services with mail or courier delivery throughout North America.

URL http://www.cyberpharmacy.com

Eli Lilly and Company

Find out about treatments for diseases such as cancer and diabetes.

URL http://www.lilly.com

Global Health Network

Worldwide resources on various health issues.

URL http://www.pitt.edu/HOME/GHNet/
GHNet.html

Medical Breakthroughs

Be informed with the up-to-date medical news at this site.

URL http://www.ivanhoe.com

National Library of Medicine

Access medical and scientific information from this huge library.

URL http://www.nlm.nih.gov/welcome.html

Nutrition Warehouse

Vitamins and nutritional supplements to help you stay healthy, build up your body or treat ailments.

URL http://www.nutrition-warehouse.com

OncoLink

Information on cancer, including causes, screening, prevention and support.

URL http://www.oncolink.upenn.edu

Solutions@disability.com

Find disability resources, products and services at this site.

URL http://disability.com

The Body

A multimedia resource on HIV and AIDS.

URL http://www.thebody.com

Virtual Hospital

Find the latest health information at this site.

URL http://indy.radiology.uiowa.edu/VirtualHospital.html

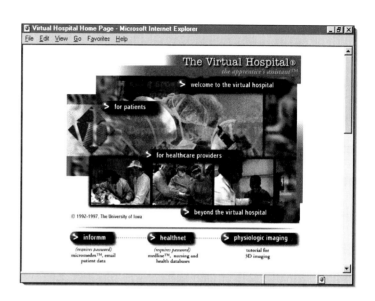

GHI

Virtual Medical Center

A large collection of medical information, as well as glossaries and dictionaries.

URL http://www-sci.lib.uci.edu/HSG/Medical.html

World Health Organization

Find out about health for everyone in the 21st Century here.

URL http://www.who.ch

HISTORY

1492: An Ongoing Voyage

This exhibit examines how the discovery of America affected nations around the world.

URL http://sunsite.unc.edu/expo/1492.exhibit/Intro.html

American Memory

This glorious site will keep an American history buff busy for days.

URL http://rs6.loc.gov/amhome.html

Genealogy Home Page

A good starting point to trace your family tree.

URL http://www.genhomepage.com

Guide to the Monarchs of England and Great Britain

Pictures and biographies of the kings and queens who have ruled Britain over the years.

URL http://www.ingress.com/~gail

History

You can quickly find historical information on any part of the world at this site.

URL http://www.arts.cuhk.hk/His.html

Labyrinth

This site provides access to information on medieval studies around the world.

URL http://www.georgetown.edu/labyrinth/labyrinth-home.html

Scrolls From the Dead Sea

Read ancient scrolls found in the caves surrounding the Dead Sea.

URL http://sunsite.unc.edu/expo/deadsea.scrolls.exhibit/intro.html

Seven Wonders of the Ancient World

Can you name all seven?

URL http://pharos.bu.edu/Egypt/Wonders

This Day in History

Learn what famous and not-so-famous events happened on this day in history.

URL http://www.historychannel.com/today

U.S. Civil War Center

Learn more about the battle between the North and South.

URL http://www.cwc.lsu.edu/civlink.htm

World War I - Trenches on the Web

An impressive collection of images and documents about the Great War.

URL http://www.worldwar1.com

WWW Medieval Resources

Links to Web sites with medieval themes.

URL http://ebbs.english.vt.edu/
medieval/medieval.ebbs.html

HTML (HYPERTEXT MARKUP LANGUAGE)

Accent Multilingual Publisher

Publish Web documents in more than 30 languages with this program.

URL http://www.accentsoft.com

Background Colors

A list of background colors available in Netscape and other browsers.

URL http://www.infi.net/wwwimages/
colorindex.html

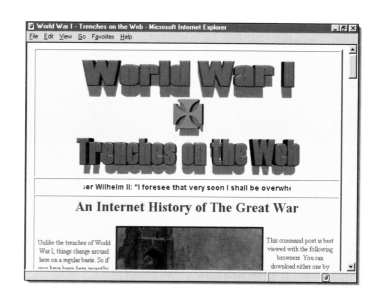

Beginner's Guide to HTML

For those who aren't quite sure what HTML is all about.

URL http://www.ncsa.uiuc.edu/General/
Internet/WWW/HTMLPrimer.html

Hot Dog Software

One of many HTML Editors.

URL http://www.sausage.com

HTML Writers Guild

The cream of the crop of HTML experts.

URL http://www.hwg.org

InterNIC

The people who keep track of North American sites on the Internet.

URL http://rs.internic.net

Java

The latest WWW programming language from Sun Microsystems.

URL http://java.sun.com

Mag's Big List of HTML Editors

The name says it all.

URL http://union.ncsa.uiuc.edu/HyperNews/
get/www/html/editors.html

Web Developer's Virtual Library

For the serious WWW page designer.

URL http://www.stars.com

WebMania!

Create Web pages incorporating forms, frames, JavaScript and more with this HTML assistant from Q&D Software.

URL http://www.q-d.com/wm.htm

HUMOR

Ask Dr. Science

Check out Dr. Science's answer to the question of the day, ask him your own question or venture into his store to buy some wacky merchandise.

URL http://www.drscience.com

Big Ron's Hedonistic Society Humor Page

This monster list of humorous sites on the Web is a comedy fan's dream come true.

URL http://www.bigron.com

Comedy Central

The all-comedy television network has a wacky site on the Web.

URL http://www.comcentral.com

Late Show Top 10 Archive

A collection of David Letterman's top ten lists.

URL http://www.cbs.com/lateshow/ttlist.html

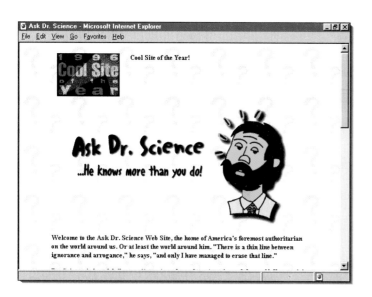

Laughter - The World's Common Language

This site finds humor in public speaking, social climbing, hosting a party and more!

URL http://www.laughter.com

LaughWEB

If the Humor Web is missing something, you can find it here.

URL http://www.intermarket.net/laughweb

Laurel & Hardy

Learn more about these masters of comedy by checking out the filmography, reviews, monthly movie listings and more.

URL http://www.ramseyltd.com/theboys

Penn & Teller

Bizarre humor with a magical twist. Be entertained by reading the Guest rant or find out where Penn & Teller will be appearing next.

URL http://www.sincity.com

Rec.Humor.Funny Home Page

Thousands of jokes and humorous stories make this site a popular hangout for cyber-comedians.

URL http://comedy.clari.net/rhf

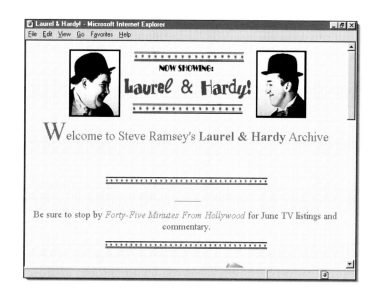

Rodney Dangerfield

Even on the Internet, he gets no respect!

URL http://www.rodney.com

INTERNET: PROGRAMS

Adobe Acrobat

A new artist-friendly WWW tool that is becoming more and more popular.

URL http://www.adobe.com/Acrobat/Acrobat0.html

Carbon Copy

Remotely control another PC with this program from Microcom-run applications, view or transfer files.

URL http://www.microcom.com/cc/ccdnload.htm

HotJava

Get a copy of HotJava, the new WWW browser created by Sun Microsystems.

URL http://java.sun.com

Internet Explorer

Microsoft's new browser for Windows 95.

URL http://www.microsoft.com/ie/default.asp

NCSA Mosaic

The first graphical browser for the WWW, the newest version of NCSA's Mosaic is available here.

URL http://www.ncsa.uiuc.edu/SDG/Software/Mosaic/NCSAMosaicHome.html

Netscape

The most popular Web browser is available here.

URL http://www.netscape.com

Pegasus Mail

A popular, free e-mail program for both networks and home computers, Pegasus offers a few cool and innovative features.

URL http://www.pegasus.usa.com

RealAudio

Get the RealAudio program and hear sound on the Internet live, without a delay.

URL http://www.realaudio.com

VocalTec

The program that may someday crush the phone companies.

URL http://www.vocaltec.com

Voxware

A cool Netscape plug-in designed to add speech to Web pages.

URL http://www.voxware.com

Worlds Inc.

The new innovative 3-D Chat program is available here.

URL http://www.worlds.net

Xing Technology

RealAudio's main competitor, Xing has developed audio and video without a delay.

URL http://www.xingtech.com

INTERNET: RESOURCES

Blazin' Bookmark

Each week, maranGraphics introduces you to one of the WWW's best sites.

URL http://www.maran.com/surf.html

Cool Science

OMNI presents a weekly list of top science sites.

URL http://www.omnimag.com/cool_science

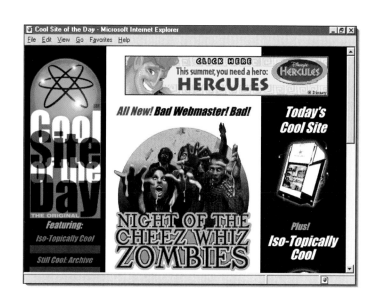

Cool Site of the Day

This popular site lists a new "cool" WWW site every day of the year.

URL http://cool.infi.net

Coolest Hostnames

Some of the stranger URLs on the Internet, like 'waiting@busstop.com'.

URL http://homepage.seas.upenn.edu/
~mengwong/coolhosts.html

Free Range Media

One of North America's top WWW design companies.

URL http://www.freerange.com

Huge List

A list of sites in many categories, including shopping, computers and sports.

URL http://thehugelist.com

IJ

Lycos Top 5%

This company reviews and rates WWW sites.

URL http://point.lycos.com/categories/
index.html

Magic URL Mystery Trip

Take a random journey through hand-picked
cool links on the Web.

URL http://www.netcreations.com/magicurl/
index.html

Mailing Lists

Browse through the available mailing lists at
this WWW site.

URL http://www.NeoSoft.com/internet/paml

Media Lab

Find out where information technology is going.

URL http://www.media.mit.edu

Project Cool Sightings

Providing a vision of coolness on the Web
every day.

URL http://www.projectcool.com/sightings

Scout Report

A weekly report of new Internet resources,
aimed at researchers and educators.

URL http://rs.internic.net/scout/report

What's Cool from Netscape

A large list of interesting sites, updated frequently.

URL http://home.netscape.com/home/
whats-cool.html

Yahoo!'s Picks of the Week

The makers of the original Web index offer a
weekly list of cool links.

URL http://www.yahoo.com/picks

JOBS

America's Job Bank

There are thousands of jobs posted here by employment offices across the country.

URL http://www.ajb.dni.us

career.com

This site connects employers and job seekers around the world. A unique feature of career.com is the virtual interviews.

URL http://www.career.com

CareerMosaic

A collection of job postings from around the world.

URL http://www.careermosaic.com/cm

CareerWEB

Find jobs from around the world, evaluate yourself with the Career Inventory or cruise the bookstore for job-related titles.

URL http://www.cweb.com

GHI

JKL

Direct Marketing World Job Center

Search for a job that's right for you.

URL http://www.dmworld.com

E-Span Employment Database

Search the database of employment ads.

URL http://www.espan.com/cgi-bin/ewais

Internet Job Center

Browse through this collection of job postings.

URL http://www.tvpress.com/jobs/
vpjic.html

JobHunt

A list of online employment resources.

URL http://www.job-hunt.org

JM

Microsoft Employment

Browse through the available positions at Microsoft.

URL http://www.microsoft.com/Jobs

NetJobs

Add a job or look one up.

URL http://www.netjobs.com

M ACINTOSH

Apple

At this site, you can find information on existing and upcoming products.

URL http://www.apple.com

Apple Internet Connection Kit

This site provides links to many interesting pages on the Web.

URL http://www.eworld.com

Apple Technical Support

Get the latest Apple software updates here.

URL http://www.support.apple.com

Claris

One of the best-known creators of Mac software.

URL http://www.claris.com

Info-Mac HyperArchive

One of the largest collections of Mac files on the Internet.

URL http://hyperarchive.lcs.mit.edu/
HyperArchive.html

Macworld Online

The online version of Macworld magazine.

URL http://www.macworld.com

Power Macintosh

The official site for information on the Power Macintosh computer.

URL http://www.info.apple.com/ppc/ ppchome.html

ULTIMATE Macintosh

This site claims to have everything a Mac user could need.

URL http://www.freepress.com/myee/ ultimate_mac.html

utexas mac archive

This huge software archive covers everything from anti-virus software to utilities.

URL http://wwwhost.ots.utexas.edu/mac/ main.html

Well Connected Mac

A site with bits and pieces of everything from periodicals to a list of mailing lists and newsgroups.

URL http://www.macfaq.com

JKL

MN

MAGAZINES

2600

A magazine dedicated to hacking and various other activities.

URL http://www.2600.com

Addicted To Noise

One of the best magazines around, this music leader often gets the scoop before Rolling Stone and Vibe.

URL http://www.addict.com/ATN

Blue Stocking

The Internet's first feminist magazine.

URL http://www.teleport.com/~bluesock

clickTV

This interactive entertainment magazine helps you get the most out of your T.V. time.

URL http://www.clickTV.com

Electronic Newsstand

This site has excerpts from many popular magazines.

URL http://www.enews.com

Gigaplex

This online magazine dedicated to arts and entertainment is full of great pictures and video.

URL http://www.gigaplex.com

HotWired

The online edition of "Wired," the magazine dedicated to media, technology and pop culture.

URL http://www.hotwired.com

Internet World

The online issues of Internet World magazine often have double the content of the print editions.

URL http://www.iw.com

Jetpack Magazine

This is a "down-to-earth" electronic publication like no other.

URL http://www.buzznet.com

Mother Jones Interactive

Mother Jones is a magazine dedicated to free thought and alternative ideas.

URL http://www.mojones.com/
motherjones.html

Pathfinder

This site includes excerpts from many magazines, including Time, People, Life and many more.

URL http://www.pathfinder.com

SALON

The magazine where politics and entertainment meet.

URL http://www.salon1999.com

t@p Online Network

A hip look at entertainment, culture, sports and technology.

URL http://www.taponline.com

Word

This electronic magazine covers a variety of issues and includes stories, news, graphics and animation.

URL http://www.word.com

Zines on-line publications

You can find many electronic magazines at this site.

URL http://www.etext.org/Zines

MOVIES

007

This site is dedicated to James Bond.

URL http://www.mcs.net/~klast/www/bond.html

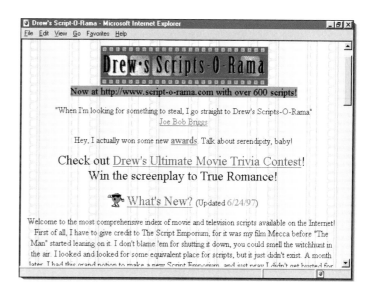

Alfred Hitchcock

Fans of "The Birds," "Vertigo" and "Psycho" should check out this site.

URL http://nextdch.mty.itesm.mx/~plopezg/Kaplan/Hitchcock.html

All-Movie Guide

Find out more about your favorite movies and actors at this searchable database.

URL http://allmovie.com/amg/movie_Root.html

Alliance On-Line

The company behind many big movies and television shows.

URL http://alliance.idirect.com

Drew's Scripts-O-Rama

You can look at more than 600 complete movie and T.V. scripts at this site.

URL http://www.script-o-rama.com

Early Motion Pictures 1897-1916

A collection of some of the earliest films made in North America.

URL http://lcweb2.loc.gov/papr/mpixhome.html

FilmZone

A great magazine with lots of informative articles on independent, foreign, animated and Hollywood films.

URL http://www.filmzone.com

Film.com

This site includes reviews of most major movies and videos.

URL http://www.film.com

Hollywood Online

A great source for information on the hottest movies and movie stars.

URL http://hollywood.com

Internet Movie Database

This free source of movie information is the largest of its kind on the Internet.

URL http://us.imdb.com

MCA/Universal

View clips of several different MCA/Universal movies.

URL http://www.mca.com

Movie Clichés List

A large collection of Hollywood clichés.

URL http://www.like.it/vertigo/cliches.html

Movie Critic

Rate movies you have already seen and find out which movies are worth seeing.

URL http://www.moviecritic.com

M.O.V.I.E. Trivia/Games

A games gallery and trivia contest where you can win prizes for your film knowledge. You can also buy M.O.V.I.E. merchandise to help support the making of independent movies.

URL http://www.moviefund.com/trivia.html

MovieLink

Find out what's playing at a theater near you.

URL http://www.movielink.com

MovieWEB

Previews of upcoming movies, movie merchandise and more.

URL http://movieweb.com

Mr. Showbiz

This site provides excellent information on the latest films.

URL http://web3.starwave.com/showbiz

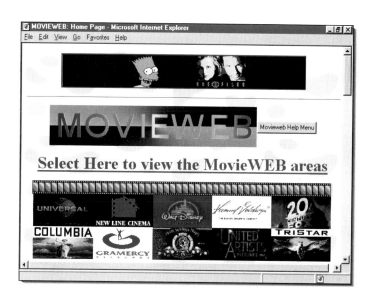

National Film Board of Canada

This award-winning group has produced many well-known Canadian films.

URL http://www.nfb.ca

Paramount Pictures

Contains information on Paramount movies and television.

URL http://www.paramount.com

Roger Ebert at the Movies

Search for this famous reviewer's opinions on films from 1985 to the present or check out the One Minute Movie Reviews of the latest releases.

URL http://www.suntimes.com/ebert/ebert.html

www.filmmusic.com

Whether you create music for films or just enjoy listening to it, this site is for you.

URL http://www.filmmusic.com

M

MUSEUMS

Andy Warhol Museum
A site dedicated to one of America's most famous artists.

URL http://www.warhol.org/warhol

Computer Museum Network
This museum includes interactive exhibits, a multimedia timeline of the history of computers and much more.

URL http://www.net.org

Exploratorium
A museum of art, science and technology.

URL http://www.exploratorium.edu

Field Museum
Browse through exhibits, learn about science and more.

URL http://www.bvis.uic.edu/museum

Franklin Institute Science Museum
This is an interactive museum where you can take quizzes, listen to sound and watch movies.

URL http://sln.fi.edu

Gallery Walk
Sample what some of the world's finest art galleries have to offer.

URL http://www.ECNet.Net/users/mfjfg/galwalk.html

Internet Arts Museum for Free
Take a tour of the museum dedicated to art, music and literature.

URL http://www.rahul.net/iamfree

Leonardo da Vinci
This site is dedicated to the famous artist and engineer.

URL http://cellini.leonardo.net/museum/main.html

Metropolitan Museum of Art

This famous New York museum displays works of art from its impressive collection.

URL http://www.metmuseum.org/htmlfile/ gallery/gallery.html

Natural History Museum

Get a taste of this British museum by previewing a few items online.

URL http://www.nhm.ac.uk

Ontario Science Centre

This site provides information on the Science Centre in Toronto, Canada.

URL http://www.osc.on.ca

Smithsonian

You can read about the many exhibits at the Smithsonian Institute.

URL http://www.si.edu

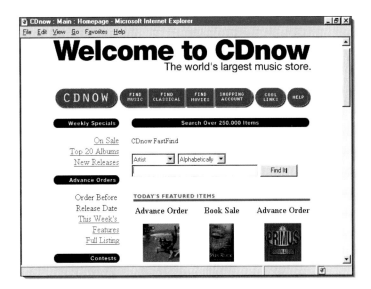

United States Holocaust Memorial Museum

A museum dedicated to the Holocaust.

URL http://www.ushmm.org

WebMuseum

The most well-known museum on the Internet.

URL http://www.emf.net/louvre

MUSIC

CDnow

You can buy your CDs online at this site.

URL http://cdnow.com

Classical Net

This site includes everything from a composer index to a beginner's guide to collecting CDs.

URL http://www.classical.net

Geffen/DGC Records

This music label is grabbing more and more hot bands.

URL http://geffen.com

Global Electronic Music Marketplace

A database of musical resources on the Internet.

URL http://gemm.com

Guitar Net

This site offers great resources for guitar enthusiasts.

URL http://www.guitar.net

Internet Underground Music Archive

This site has become a big hit with experienced Internet users. It offers information on all types of music, from heavy metal to easy listening.

URL http://www.iuma.com

Jazz Online

If you're not into rock music, Jazz Online offers a fresh alternative.

URL http://www.jazzonln.com

L.A. Philharmonic

Symphony music fans will enjoy the Los Angeles Philharmonic's home on the Internet.

URL http://www.laphil.org

Music Boulevard

Take a walk down the Boulevard to find a large selection of music titles, as well as contests, music news and more.

URL http://www.musicblvd.com

PolyGram Online

Find information on your favorite band and even listen to sound clips.

URL http://www.polygram.com/polygram

Rock and Roll Hall of Fame

This music museum in Cleveland has an A+ site.

URL http://www.rockhall.com

Rock Online

Find information on the latest artists, listen to unreleased songs and more at this site.

URL http://www.rockonline.com/emi

Roughstock's History of Country Music

A great presentation of country music history from the 1930s to the present. Be sure to check out the images, sounds and digital movies.

URL http://www.roughstock.com/history

Sony Online

Read about Michael Jackson, Mariah Carey, Michael Bolton and lots of other artists.

URL http://www.sony.com

TicketMaster Online

Find out when your favorite band is coming to town.

URL U.S.   http://www.ticketmaster.com
URL Canada   http://www.ticketmaster.ca

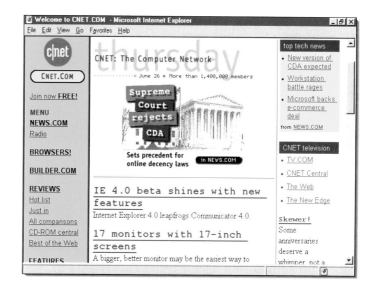

Warner Bros. Records

Like the Sony site, Warner lets you browse through information on your favorite artists.

URL http://www.iuma.com/warner

N EWS

CNET: The Computer Network

The online site of CNET, the weekly computer show on cable.

URL http://www.cnet.com

ClariNet Communications Corp.

A popular service that provides news via newsgroups.

URL http://www.clarinet.com

CNN

CNN is one of the world's most popular all-news television networks. This site is full of articles, updates and video clips.

URL http://www.cnn.com

Comic Strip

Read comic strips that appear in newspapers nationwide.

URL http://www.unitedmedia.com/comics

National Public Radio

A schedule of news programming on National Public Radio.

URL http://www.npr.org

New York Times Fax

An online, condensed version of the New York Times.

URL http://nytimesfax.com

NewsPage

NewsPage provides you with current, pre-sorted news across a broad array of topics and industries.

URL http://www.newspage.com

Top 100 Newspapers

This great site provides links to the Top 100 newspapers in the country.

URL http://www.interest.com/top100.html

USA Today

This site has all of the latest news and, for now, is offered for free to the public.

URL http://www.usatoday.com

Yahoo! News

Up-to-the-minute news, entertainment, sports and much more.

URL http://www.yahoo.com/headlines/current

Religion

Bible Gateway

Search the Bible in many different languages.

URL http://www.gospelcom.net/bible

BuddhaNet

This site provides answers to common questions about Buddhism.

URL http://www2.hawkesbury.uws.edu.au/
BuddhaNet

Christus Rex et Redemptor Mundi

A collection of Christian information and writings.

URL http://www.christusrex.org

Islam Page

A directory of Islamic sites on the Web.

URL http://www.wam.umd.edu/~ibrahim

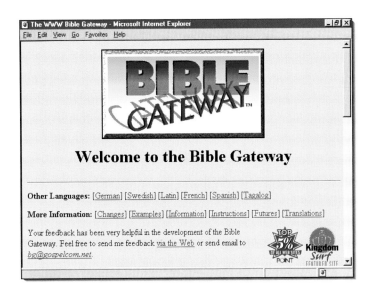

Jerusalem Mosaic

Take a virtual tour of Jerusalem.

URL http://www1.huji.ac.il/jeru/
jerusalem.html

Monastery of Christ in the Desert

A group of monks in the Santa Fe desert have their own Web site.

URL http://www.christdesert.org

Scrolls From the Dead Sea

Browse through an exhibit of ancient scrolls.

URL http://sunsite.unc.edu/expo/
deadsea.scrolls.exhibit/intro.html

Secular Web

A source of information for atheists.

URL http://freethought.tamu.edu

R S

Shamash

A site dedicated to serving Jewish people on the Internet.

URL http://shamash.nysernet.org

Sikhism Home Page

A guide to a popular Eastern religion.

URL http://www.sikhs.org

SEARCH TOOLS

AltaVista

Quickly search millions of Web pages and thousands of newsgroups.

URL http://altavista.digital.com

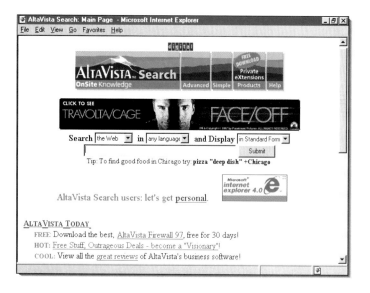

DejaNews

A tool for searching newsgroup articles.

URL http://www.dejanews.com

Excite

Excite lets you search for information using a phrase of key words.

URL http://www.excite.com

Four11

Looking for someone on the Internet? Visit Four11 and access more than 6.5 million e-mail addresses.

URL http://www.four11.com

Galaxy

An Internet directory with a smaller selection of topics than Yahoo.

URL http://www.einet.net

infoseek

A commercial Internet search tool that offers free trial accounts.

URL http://www.infoseek.com

Lycos

Located at Carnegie Mellon University, this is one of the top Internet search tools in the world.

URL http://www.lycos.com

Magellan Internet Guide

The McKinley Group presents this well-indexed guide to the Web.

URL http://www.mckinley.com

Open Text Index

A well-established search tool for the Web that allows for complicated searches, such as "ketchup and mustard but not relish."

URL http://index.opentext.net

SavvySearch

SavvySearch sends your inquiry to many different search tools around the world.

URL http://www.cs.colostate.edu/~dreiling/smartform.html

WebCrawler

An Internet search tool sponsored by America Online.

URL http://webcrawler.com

What's New with NCSA Mosaic

NCSA lists most of the new sites on the Web and is updated 3 times a week.

URL http://www.ncsa.uiuc.edu/SDG/Software/Mosaic/Docs/whats-new.html

WhoWhere?

Need to know someone's e-mail address? Check out this useful site.

URL http://www.whowhere.com

World Wide Web Worm

This search tool won a Best of the Web '94 award.

URL http://www.cs.colorado.edu/home/mcbryan/WWWW.html

RS

WWW Virtual Library

A catalog with a wide variety of Web sites.

URL http://www.w3.org/hypertext/DataSources/
bySubject/Overview.html

Yahoo!

The ever-popular Internet directory.

URL http://www.yahoo.com

SPORTS

Broomball

All you ever wanted to know about broomball.

URL http://www.ozemail.com.au/~kshapley

CFL

At this site, you will find statistics, scores,
schedules and much more.

URL http://www.cfl.ca

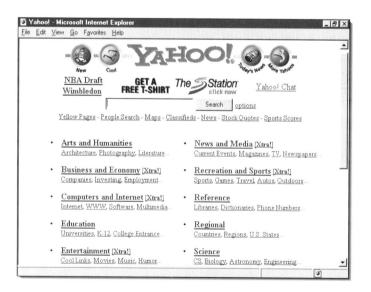

CSC College Sports Internet Channel

This site features numerous links to up-to-date
information on college sports.

URL http://www.xcscx.com/colsport

DiveNet

World Wide Divers' Network.

URL http://divenet.com

ESPNET SportsZone

This site provides all a sports fan could want:
scores, pictures, schedules and more.

URL http://espnet.sportszone.com

GolfWeb

A complete golf information service.

URL http://www.golfweb.com

LiveSt@ts

Ever wish you had complete statistics at your fingertips while you watch the game? LiveSt@ts gives you all the stats you need.

URL http://www.livestats.com

NBA

Find information on your favorite teams and players from the NBA.

URL http://www.nba.com

NBC Sports

NBC brings its quality sports reporting to the Web.

URL http://www.nbc.com/sports/index.html

NHL Official Site

At this site, you will find schedules, contests and the latest news.

URL http://www.nhl.com

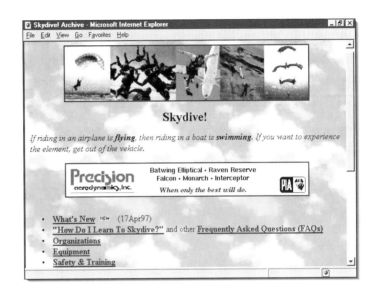

NHLPA

The National Hockey League Players' Association provides statistics and information on players.

URL http://www.nhlpa.com

Online Sports

This site is both a directory and showplace of sports products and services available online and also has a sports career center.

URL http://www.onlinesports.com

Skydive!

Like bungee jumping, but without the bungee.

URL http://www.afn.org/skydive

SportSite

Several different forums on areas of sports such as cycling, skiing and camping.

URL http://www.sportsite.com

RS

Surfing News

The latest news from the surfing world, including tournament standings, global surf links and more.

URL http://holoholo.org/surfnews

TSN

You can find scores and standings for many major sports at this site.

URL http://www.tsn.ca

USA Today Sports

Find the top sports stories from USA Today.

URL http://www.usatoday.com/sports/sfront.htm

USGA

The United States Golf Association features real-time scores during major golf tournaments, as well as a huge collection of golf information.

URL http://www.usga.org

VeloNews Interactive

A well-designed site covering everything about the world of bicycle racing.

URL http://www.velonews.com

Volleyball World Wide

Bump, set, spike, surf.

URL http://www.volleyball.org

TELEVISION

Academy of Television Arts & Sciences

The official site of the Emmys.

URL http://www.emmys.org

Amazing Discoveries

The infomercials we can't resist.

URL http://www.AmazingDiscoveries.com

BBC

Find out what the British are watching on TV and listening to on the radio.

URL http://www.bbc.co.uk

Black Entertainment Television

Television programming focusing on the African-American population.

URL http://www.betnetworks.com

CBC

Find out what's on Canadian television and radio.

URL http://www.cbc.ca

CBS Eye on the Net

CBS was the first of the three big networks to go online.

URL http://www.cbs.com

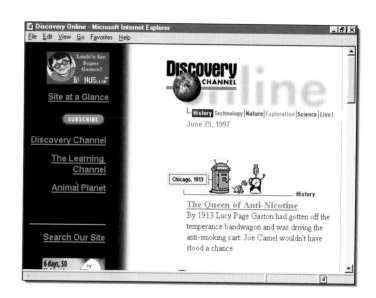

CNN Interactive

CNN is one of the world's most popular all-news television networks. This site is full of articles, updates and video clips.

URL http://www.cnn.com

Comedy Central

The nutty cable channel has its own Web site full of laughs.

URL http://www.comcentral.com

CourtTV Law Center

All trials, all the time.

URL http://www.courttv.com

Discovery Channel

The Canadian and American branches of the Discovery Channel each have their own Web site.

URL U.S.   http://www.discovery.com
URL Canada   http://www.discovery.ca

FOX World

This site has information on shows such as
The X-Files, Melrose Place and The Simpsons.

URL http://www.foxnetwork.com

iQVC Shop

The home-shopping channel. QVC features
a bus-ride theme with stops to visit the hosts
and see the featured products of the week.

URL http://www.qvc.com

Late Show with David Letterman

This site includes a collection of Dave's
Top Ten lists.

URL http://www.cbs.com/lateshow

MTV Online

MTV's site provides great graphics and
a schedule of programs.

URL http://www.mtv.com

MuchMusic

Canada's equivalent of MTV.

URL http://www.muchmusic.com/
muchmusic

NBC

Find information on popular NBC shows such
as Frasier, Friends, Seinfeld and more.

URL http://www.nbc.com

PBS Online

Check out the latest programs, visit the online
store and much more at this site.

URL http://www.pbs.org

Ricki Lake

The official site for Ricki Lake's popular talk show.

URL http://www.spe.sony.com/Pictures/tv/
rickilake/ricki.html

Sci-Fi Channel

Nicknamed "The Dominion," this site has information on the Sci-Fi channel and science-fiction in general.

URL http://www.scifi.com

Showtime Online

Find information, reviews and schedules for this large cable network.

URL http://showtimeonline.com

Simpsons Archive

Homer, Marge, Bart, Lisa and Maggie.

URL http://www.digimark.net/
TheSimpsons/index.html

Star Trek

The most popular television program on the Internet.

URL http://www.holodeck3.com
URL http://startrek.msn.com

Tonight Show with Jay Leno

This site is updated every day with the latest jokes and scheduled guests.

URL http://www.nbctonightshow.com

Travel Channel

Get away from it all. This site offers travel tips and expert advice as well as program information.

URL http://www.travelchannel.com

Ultimate TV

If you are looking for a Web site for a particular program, look no further.

URL http://www.ultimatetv.com

Weather Channel

Weather reports from around the U.S. as well as a new piece of weather trivia each day.

URL http://www.weather.com

TU

X-Files

This popular television show has many sites on the Web with pictures, sound and information.

URL http://www.thex-files.com

Young and the Restless

A fact-filled site with many pictures and even the theme song from the soap.

URL http://www.youngandtherestless.com

THEATER

Andrew Lloyd Webber

Learn about Sir Andrew himself, read up on his famous musicals like Cats and Phantom of the Opera or hear recordings online.

URL http://www.reallyuseful.com

Dramatic Exchange

A place to review the works of playwrights.

URL http://www.dramex.org

Gilbert & Sullivan Archive

Find information on musicals like H.M.S. Pinafore.

URL http://diamond.idbsu.edu/gas/GaS.html

Kabuki for Everyone

Learn more about this traditional Japanese form of theater through the pictures, sounds and movies presented here.

URL http://www.fix.co.jp/kabuki/kabuki.html

Les Misérables

This site has information about the musical based on the famous French novel.

URL http://www.ot.com/lesmis

Musicals Home Page

Song lists, music samples and even pictures of CD covers from your favorite musicals.

URL http://musical.mit.edu/musical

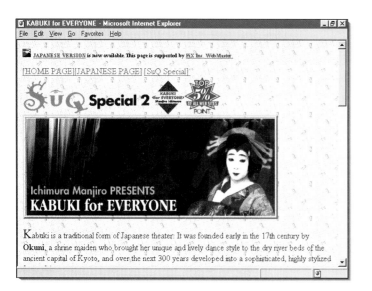

On Broadway

A list of the shows currently playing in the Big Apple.

URL http://artsnet.heinz.cmu.edu:80/ OnBroadway

Playbill Online

A great source of theater news, information and trivia from the company that creates the programs for most Broadway shows.

URL http://www.webcom.com/~broadway

Screenwriters & Playwrights

All kinds of resources for all kinds of writers.

URL http://www.teleport.com/~cdeemer/ scrwriter.html

Shakespeare Web

A good place to start if you want to learn more about Shakespeare.

URL http://www.shakespeare.com

Talent Network

An online talent agency.

URL http://www.talentnet.com

Theatre Central

Your one-stop guide to theater on the Internet, complete with job listings, professional contacts and links to other theater related sites.

URL http://www.theatre-central.com

TRAVEL

American Airlines

Find flight schedules, information and much more at this site.

URL http://www.amrcorp.com

Epicurious Travel

A guide to trips around the world.

URL http://travel.epicurious.com

TU

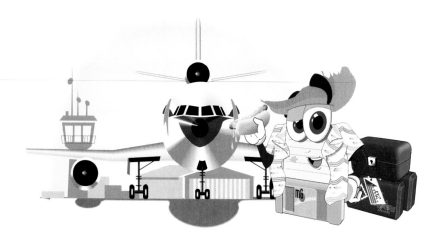

Reed Travel Group

Information on destinations in the U.S. and around the world.

URL http://www.traveler.net

Southwest Airlines

Find information on the cities Southwest flies to, learn how to pack smart and more at this site.

URL http://www.iflyswa.com

Subway Navigator

How to get from A to B via the subway in over 50 cities around the world.

URL http://metro.jussieu.fr:10001/bin/ cities/english

Switzerland

Information on the land known for its neutrality.

URL http://heiwww.unige.ch/switzerland

Travel Channel

Browse the globe with a click of a button.

URL http://www.travelchannel.com

Travel Source

A huge travel guide with everything from airlines to yacht charters.

URL http://www.travelsource.com

Travel Warnings & Consular Information Sheets

This site provides travel information for countries around the world. It also lets you know which countries to avoid due to disease, war and natural disasters.

URL http://travel.state.gov/travel_warnings.html

Web Travel Review

First-hand accounts from people who have travelled to countries around the world.

URL http://webtravel.org/webtravel

WINDOWS

Microsoft

The giant company behind Windows.

URL http://www.microsoft.com

Microsoft Network

Information on The Microsoft Network and the Internet.

URL http://www.msn.com

Windows Internet Magazine

An online Windows publication with a computer buyer's guide, online shopping listings and other neat features.

URL http://www.winmag.com

Windows Software

Where to find Windows software on the Internet.

URL http://www.nova.edu/Inter-Links/software/windows.html

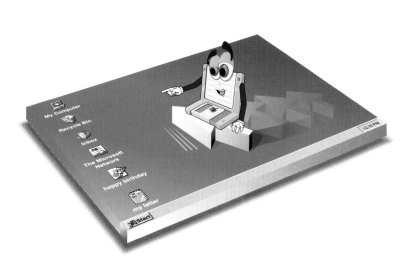

Windows95.com

An excellent site with a huge amount of Windows 95 information, drivers and programs.

URL http://www.windows95.com

WINGate Technologies

This company creates software to enable communications between Windows and DOS applications.

URL http://www.wingate.com

WinSite Archive

A searchable collection of Windows software for almost anything you could want, from Web page design programs to an insult generator.

URL http://www.winsite.com

WinZip

The home page of the award-winning file compression program for Windows.

URL http://www.winzip.com

TU

VW

INDEX

A

abbreviations, e-mail, 64
access, high-speed, 14
ActiveX, 43
addresses
    books, e-mail, 68
    e-mail, 62-63
        finding, 63
    mailing lists, 80
    Web, 27
AltaVista, 48
America Online (AOL), 20. *See also* commercial online services
animals, Web site on, 146-147
animation, 37
anonymous FTP sites, 122
applet, Java, 40-41
applications. *See* programs on Internet
Archie, 129
archived files, 128
ARPANET, 10
art, Web site on, 147-149
articles
    newsgroups, 91, 96-97
    sorting, 91
astronomy, Web site on, 149
at signs (@) in e-mail addresses, 62
automated mailing lists, 82
Automatic Information Retrieval (AIR), 14

B

backbone, 13
banking on Web, 35
beta versions, Web browsers, 29
biology, Web site on, 150
bizarre, Web site on, 151-153
blind carbon copies of e-mail messages, 66
bookmarks, 29
books and language, Web site on, 153-155
bounced e-mail messages, 69
browsers, Web. *See* Web browsers
business: companies, Web site on, 155-157
business: finance, Web site on, 158-159
business: shopping, Web site on, 160-161
busy signals
    on freenets, 17
    on ISPs, 18

C

carbon copies of e-mail messages, 66
cars, Web site on, 161-163
channels, chat, 109
    IRC, examples, 118-119
    operators, chat, 109
chat
    via commercial online services, 21
    overview, 106-107
    3-D, 115
    video, 117
    voice, 116
    Web-based, 114-115
chemistry, Web site on, 163-164
cloning, chat, 113
commercial online services, 17, 20-21
    chat, 21
    cost, 20
    help, 21
    information, 21
commercial software games, 142-143
companies: business, Web site on, 155-157
compression
    e-mail, attached files, 67
    files, 67
    SLIP (CSLIP), 19
CompuServe, 20. *See also* commercial online services
computers: pictures, Web site on, 164-166
computers: resources, Web site on, 166-167
computers: sounds, Web site on, 168-169
connecting to Internet
    via commercial online services, 20-21
    computers for, 16
    via freenets, 17
    via Internet service providers, 18-19
    modems for, 16
    password, 17
    service for, 17, 18-21
    software for, 16
    user name, 17
    ways to, 17
conversation, online. *See* chat
credit cards, using on Web, 35
Crescendo, 31
cyberspace, 4. *See also* Internet

D

dance and dance music, Web site on, 170-171
decompression, files, 128
digests, 81

INDEX

governments and information on the world, Web site on, 182-183
graphics. *See* images

H

health, Web site on, 183-185
help
    commercial online services, 21
    Internet service providers, 19
helper programs, 73
high-speed access, Internet, 14
history lists, 29
history, Web site on, 185-187
HTML (HyperText Markup Language), 46
    Web site on, 187-188
http (HyperText Transfer Protocol), 27
humor, Web site on, 188-189
hypertext, 27

I

images
    at FTP sites, 124
    on Web, 52
information
    available on Internet, 6
    as commercial online service feature, 21
    download from Internet, 13
    transfer explained, 12-13
    on the U.S., Web site on, 180-182
    on the world, Web site on, 182-183
Information Superhighway, 4. *See also* Internet
Internet. *See also specific subject*
    access, 21
    chat. *See* chat
    connecting to, 16-21. *See also* connecting to Internet
    Explorer, Microsoft, 16. *See also* Web browsers
    future, 14-15
    history, 10-11
    information, 6-7, 38-39
        free, providers of, 9
        transfer explained, 12-13
    overview, 4-5
    payment for, 8-9
    service providers, 22-23
    television terminals, 56-57
Internet Explorer, Microsoft, 16. *See also* Web browsers
Internet: programs, Web site on, 189-191
Internet Relay Chat. *See* IRC
Internet: resources, Web site on, 191-192
IP (Internet Protocol), 12
IRC (Internet Relay Chat)
    channels, examples, 118-119

    etiquette, 112-113
    networks, 110
    overview, 108-109
    programs, 111
ISPs (Internet Service Providers), 17, 18-19

J

Java, 40-41
JavaScript, 42
jobs, Web site on, 193-194

K

kill files, newsgroups, 93

L

language and books, Web site on, 153-155
links in Web pages, 53
    checking, 53
    exchanging, 55
lurking, 101
Lycos, 49

M

Macintosh, Web site on, 194-195
magazines, Web site on, 195-197
mail, electronic. *See* e-mail
mailing lists
    addresses, 80
    automated, 82
    digests, 81
    etiquette, 84-85
    examples, 86-87
    manually maintained, 82
    moderated, 83
    overview, 78
    quoting, 85
    restricted, 83
    subscribing, 80-81
    unsubscribing, 80
manually maintained mailing lists, 82
messages. *See* chat; e-mail; mailing lists; newsgroups
Microsoft Internet Explorer, 16. *See also* Web browsers
Microsoft Network (The), 20. *See also* commercial online services
MIME (Multi-purpose Internet Mail Extensions), 67
mirror sites, 126
modems, 16
    speed, 16
moderated mailing lists, 83
moderated newsgroups, 94

INDEX

Y

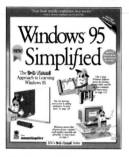

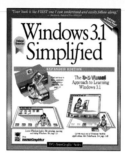

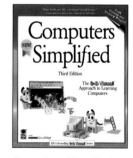

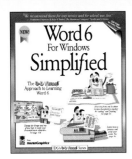

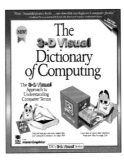
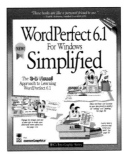

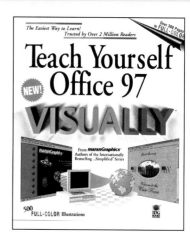

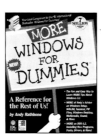

Title	Author	ISBN #	Price
INTERNET/COMMUNICATIONS/NETWORKING			
CompuServe For Dummies™	by Wallace Wang	ISBN: 1-56884-181-7	$19.95 USA/$26.95 Canada
Modems For Dummies™, 2nd Edition	by Tina Rathbone	ISBN: 1-56884-223-6	$19.99 USA/$26.99 Canada
Modems For Dummies™	by Tina Rathbone	ISBN: 1-56884-001-2	$19.95 USA/$26.95 Canada
MORE Internet For Dummies™	by John Levine & Margaret Levine Young	ISBN: 1-56884-164-7	$19.95 USA/$26.95 Canada
NetWare For Dummies™	by Ed Tittel & Deni Connor	ISBN: 1-56884-003-9	$19.95 USA/$26.95 Canada
Networking For Dummies™	by Doug Lowe	ISBN: 1-56884-079-9	$19.95 USA/$26.95 Canada
ProComm Plus 2 For Windows For Dummies™	by Wallace Wang	ISBN: 1-56884-219-8	$19.99 USA/$26.99 Canada
The Internet Help Desk For Dummies™	by John Kaufeld	ISBN: 1-56884-238-4	$16.99 USA/$22.99 Canada
The3 Internet For Dummies™, 2nd Edition	by John Levine & Carol Baroudi	ISBN: 1-56884-222-8	$19.99 USA/$26.99 Canada
The Internet For Macs For Dummies™	by Charles Seiter	ISBN: 1-56884-184-1	$19.95 USA/$26.95 Canada
MACINTOSH			
Mac Programming For Dummies™	by Dan Parks Sydow	ISBN: 1-56884-173-6	$19.95 USA/$26.95 Canada
Macintosh System 7.5 For Dummies™	by Bob LeVitus	ISBN: 1-56884-197-3	$19.95 USA/$26.95 Canada
MORE Macs For Dummies™	by David Pogue	ISBN: 1-56884-087-X	$19.95 USA/$26.95 Canada
PageMaker 5 For Macs For Dummies™	by Galen Gruman & Deke McClelland	ISBN: 1-56884-178-7	$19.95 USA/$26.95 Canada
QuarkXPress 3.3 For Dummies™	by Galen Gruman & Barbara Assadi	ISBN: 1-56884-217-1	$19.99 USA/$26.99 Canada
Upgrading and Fixing Macs For Dummies™	by Kearney Rietmann & Frank Higgins	ISBN: 1-56884-189-2	$19.95 USA/$26.95 Canada
MULTIMEDIA			
Multimedia & CD-ROMs For Dummies™, Interactive Multimedia Value Pack	by Andy Rathbone	ISBN: 1-56884-225-2	$29.95 USA/$39.95 Canada
Multimedia & CD-ROMs For Dummies™	by Andy Rathbone	ISBN: 1-56884-089-6	$19.95 USA/$26.95 Canada
OPERATING SYSTEMS/DOS			
MORE DOS For Dummies™	by Dan Gookin	ISBN: 1-56884-046-2	$19.95 USA/$26.95 Canada
S.O.S. For DOS™	by Katherine Murray	ISBN: 1-56884-043-8	$12.95 USA/$16.95 Canada
OS/2 For Dummies™	by Andy Rathbone	ISBN: 1-878058-76-2	$19.95 USA/$26.95 Canada
UNIX			
UNIX For Dummies™	by John Levine & Margaret Levine Young	ISBN: 1-878058-58-4	$19.95 USA/$26.95 Canada
WINDOWS			
S.O.S. For Windows™	by Katherine Murray	ISBN: 1-56884-045-4	$12.95 USA/$16.95 Canada
Windows "X" For Dummies™, 3rd Edition	by Andy Rathbone	ISBN: 1-56884-240-6	$19.99 USA/$26.99 Canada
PCS/HARDWARE			
Illustrated Computer Dictionary For Dummies™	by Dan Gookin, Wally Wang, & Chris Van Buren	ISBN: 1-56884-004-7	$12.95 USA/$16.95 Canada
Upgrading and Fixing PCs For Dummies™	by Andy Rathbone	ISBN: 1-56884-002-0	$19.95 USA/$26.95 Canada
PRESENTATION/AUTOCAD			
AutoCAD For Dummies™	by Bud Smith	ISBN: 1-56884-191-4	$19.95 USA/$26.95 Canada
PowerPoint 4 For Windows For Dummies™	by Doug Lowe	ISBN: 1-56884-161-2	$16.95 USA/$22.95 Canada
PROGRAMMING			
Borland C++ For Dummies™	by Michael Hyman	ISBN: 1-56884-162-0	$19.95 USA/$26.95 Canada
"Borland's New Language Product" For Dummies™	by Neil Rubenking	ISBN: 1-56884-200-7	$19.95 USA/$26.95 Canada
C For Dummies™	by Dan Gookin	ISBN: 1-878058-78-9	$19.95 USA/$26.95 Canada
C++ For Dummies™	by S. Randy Davis	ISBN: 1-56884-163-9	$19.95 USA/$26.95 Canada
Mac Programming For Dummies™	by Dan Parks Sydow	ISBN: 1-56884-173-6	$19.95 USA/$26.95 Canada
QBasic Programming For Dummies™	by Douglas Hergert	ISBN: 1-56884-093-4	$19.95 USA/$26.95 Canada
Visual Basic "X" For Dummies™, 2nd Edition	by Wallace Wang	ISBN: 1-56884-230-9	$19.99 USA/$26.99 Canada
Visual Basic 3 For Dummies™	by Wallace Wang	ISBN: 1-56884-076-4	$19.95 USA/$26.95 Canada
SPREADSHEET			
1-2-3 For Dummies™	by Greg Harvey	ISBN: 1-878058-60-6	$16.95 USA/$22.95 Canada
1-2-3 For Windows 5 For Dummies™, 2nd Edition	by John Walkenbach	ISBN: 1-56884-216-3	$16.95 USA/$22.95 Canada
1-2-3 For Windows For Dummies™	by John Walkenbach	ISBN: 1-56884-052-7	$16.95 USA/$22.95 Canada
Excel 5 For Macs For Dummies™	by Greg Harvey	ISBN: 1-56884-186-8	$19.95 USA/$26.95 Canada
Excel For Dummies™, 2nd Edition	by Greg Harvey	ISBN: 1-56884-050-0	$16.95 USA/$22.95 Canada
MORE Excel 5 For Windows For Dummies™	by Greg Harvey	ISBN: 1-56884-207-4	$19.95 USA/$26.95 Canada
Quattro Pro 6 For Windows For Dummies™	by John Walkenbach	ISBN: 1-56884-174-4	$19.95 USA/$26.95 Canada
Quattro Pro For DOS For Dummies™	by John Walkenbach	ISBN: 1-56884-023-3	$16.95 USA/$22.95 Canada
UTILITIES			
Norton Utilities 8 For Dummies™	by Beth Slick	ISBN: 1-56884-166-3	$19.95 USA/$26.95 Canada
VCRS/CAMCORDERS			
VCRs & Camcorders For Dummies™	by Andy Rathbone & Gordon McComb	ISBN: 1-56884-229-5	$14.99 USA/$20.99 Canada
WORD PROCESSING			
Ami Pro For Dummies™	by Jim Meade	ISBN: 1-56884-049-7	$19.95 USA/$26.95 Canada
More Word For Windows 6 For Dummies™	by Doug Lowe	ISBN: 1-56884-165-5	$19.95 USA/$26.95 Canada
MORE WordPerfect 6 For Windows For Dummies™	by Margaret Levine Young & David C. Kay	ISBN: 1-56884-206-6	$19.95 USA/$26.95 Canada
MORE WordPerfect 6 For DOS For Dummies™	by Wallace Wang, edited by Dan Gookin	ISBN: 1-56884-047-0	$19.95 USA/$26.95 Canada
S.O.S. For WordPerfect™	by Katherine Murray	ISBN: 1-56884-053-5	$12.95 USA/$16.95 Canada
Word 6 For Macs For Dummies™	by Dan Gookin	ISBN: 1-56884-190-6	$19.95 USA/$26.95 Canada
Word For Windows 6 For Dummies™	by Dan Gookin	ISBN: 1-56884-075-6	$16.95 USA/$22.95 Canada
Word For Windows 2 For Dummies™	by Dan Gookin	ISBN: 1-878058-86-X	$16.95 USA/$22.95 Canada
WordPerfect 6 For Dummies™	by Dan Gookin	ISBN: 1-878058-77-0	$16.95 USA/$22.95 Canada
WordPerfect For Dummies™	by Dan Gookin	ISBN: 1-878058-52-5	$16.95 USA/$22.95 Canada
WordPerfect For Windows For Dummies™	by Margaret Levine Young & David C. Kay	ISBN: 1-56884-032-2	$16.95 USA/$22.95 Canada

IDG BOOKS ®

TRADE & INDIVIDUAL ORDERS

Phone: **(800) 762-2974**
or **(317) 895-5200**
(8 a.m.–6 p.m., CST, week-days)FAX : **(317) 895-5298**

EDUCATIONAL ORDERS & DISCOUNTS

Phone: **(800) 434-2086**
(8:30 a.m.–5:00 p.m., CST, week-days)FAX : **(817) 251-8174**

CORPORATE ORDERS FOR 3-D VISUAL™ SERIES

Phone: **(800) 469-6616**
(8 a.m.–5 p.m., EST, weekdays)
FAX : **(905) 890-9434**

Qty	ISBN	Title	Price	Total

Shipping & Handling Charges

	Description	First book	Each add'l. book	Total
Domestic	Normal	$4.50	$1.50	$
	Two Day Air	$8.50	$2.50	$
	Overnight	$18.00	$3.00	$
International	Surface	$8.00	$8.00	$
	Airmail	$16.00	$16.00	$
	DHL Air	$17.00	$17.00	$

Subtotal _____

CA residents add applicable sales tax _____

IN, MA and MD residents add 5% sales tax _____

IL residents add 6.25% sales tax _____

RI residents add 7% sales tax _____

TX residents add 8.25% sales tax _____

Shipping _____

Total _____

Ship to:

Name_____

Address_____

Company_____

City/State/Zip_____

Daytime Phone_____

Payment: ☐ Check to IDG Books (US Funds Only)
☐ Visa ☐ Mastercard ☐ American Express

Card # _____ Exp. _____ Signature_____

maranGraphics™

IDG BOOKS WORLDWIDE REGISTRATION CARD

Visit our
Web site at
http://www.idgbooks.com

ISBN Number: 0-7645-6029-8

Title of this book: Internet & World Wide Web Simplified®, 2E

My overall rating of this book: ❏ Very good [1]   ❏ Good [2]   ❏ Satisfactory [3]   ❏ Fair [4]   ❏ Poor [5]

How I first heard about this book:

❏ Found in bookstore; name: [6]   ❏ Book review: [7]

❏ Advertisement: [8]   ❏ Catalog: [9]

❏ Word of mouth; heard about book from friend, co-worker, etc.: [10]   ❏ Other: [11]

What I liked most about this book:

What I would change, add, delete, etc., in future editions of this book:

Other comments:

Number of computer books I purchase in a year: ❏ 1 [12]   ❏ 2-5 [13]   ❏ 6-10 [14]   ❏ More than 10 [15]

I would characterize my computer skills as: ❏ Beginner [16]   ❏ Intermediate [17]   ❏ Advanced [18]   ❏ Professional [19]

I use ❏ DOS [20]   ❏ Windows [21]   ❏ OS/2 [22]   ❏ Unix [23]   ❏ Macintosh [24]   ❏ Other: [25]_____

(please specify)

I would be interested in new books on the following subjects:
(please check all that apply, and use the spaces provided to identify specific software)

❏ Word processing: [26]   ❏ Spreadsheets: [27]

❏ Data bases: [28]   ❏ Desktop publishing: [29]

❏ File Utilities: [30]   ❏ Money management: [31]

❏ Networking: [32]   ❏ Programming languages: [33]

❏ Other: [34]

I use a PC at (please check all that apply): ❏ home [35]   ❏ work [36]   ❏ school [37]   ❏ other: [38]_____

The disks I prefer to use are ❏ 5.25 [39]   ❏ 3.5 [40]   ❏ other: [41]_____

I have a CD ROM: ❏ yes [42]   ❏ no [43]

I plan to buy or upgrade computer hardware this year: ❏ yes [44]   ❏ no [45]

I plan to buy or upgrade computer software this year: ❏ yes [46]   ❏ no [47]

Name: Business title: [48]   Type of Business: [49]

Address (❏ home [50] ❏ work [51]/Company name: _____)

Street/Suite#

City [52]/State [53]/Zip code [54]:   Country [55]

❏ **I liked this book!** You may quote me by name in future
IDG Books Worldwide promotional materials.

My daytime phone number is _____

IDG
BOOKS
WORLDWIDE
THE WORLD OF
COMPUTER
KNOWLEDGE®

❏ YES!

Please keep me informed about IDG Books Worldwide's World of Computer Knowledge. Send me your latest catalog.

BESTSELLING BOOK SERIES FROM IDG

TECHNICAL BOOKS